FROM THOSE WONDERFUL FOLKS WHO GAVE YOU PEARL HARBOR

Front-Line Dispatches from the Advertising War

Jerry Della Femina
Edited by Charles Sopkin

JERICHO PUBLIC LIBRARY

SIMON & SCHUSTER PAPERBACKS
New York   London   Toronto   Sydney

Simon & Schuster Paperbacks
A Division of Simon & Schuster, Inc.
1230 Avenue of the Americas
New York, NY 10020

Introduction copyright © 2010 by Jerry Della Femina
Copyright © 1970 by Jerry Della Femina and Charles Sopkin
Copyright renewed © 1998

All rights reserved, including the right to reproduce this book or portions thereof in any form whatsoever. For information address Simon & Schuster Paperbacks Subsidiary Rights Department, 1230
Avenue of the Americas, New York, NY 10020.

First Simon & Schuster trade paperback edition July 2010

SIMON & SCHUSTER PAPERBACKS and colophon are registered trademarks of Simon & Schuster, Inc.

For information about special discounts for bulk purchases, please contact Simon & Schuster Special
Sales at 1-866-506-1949 or business@simonandschuster.com.

The Simon & Schuster Speakers Bureau can bring authors to your live event. For more information
or to book an event, contact the Simon & Schuster Speakers Bureau at 1-866-248-3049 or visit our
website at www.simonspeakers.com.

Manufactured in the United States of America

10 9 8 7 6 5 4 3 2 1

Library of Congress Cataloging-in-Publication Data is available.

ISBN 978-1-4516-0990-5
ISBN 978-1-4516-0994-3 (ebook)

This book is dedicated to the dedicated: Ally, Bernbach, Burnett, Calet, Case, Dunst, Durfee, Frankfurt, Gage, Goldschmidt, Harper, Hirsch, Karsch, Kurnit, Lois, McCabe, Moss, Paccione, Raboy, Rosenfeld, Travisano, Wells and all the others.

Author's Note

The advertising business is, if nothing else, highly volatile. Factual references, billings, account affiliations at agencies and other similar details are accurate, to the best of our knowledge, as of October 1, 1969. Undoubtedly, accounts will move and billings will change between the time this book goes into production and publication day. If there are any such errors, the author and editor regret them. One final note: To protect the innocent and guilty alike, a few pseudonyms have been used in the book, but $99^{44}/_{100}$ per cent of the names, agencies and situations described are real.

FROM THOSE WONDERFUL FOLKS WHO GAVE YOU PEARL HARBOR

INTRODUCTION
JERRY DELLA FEMINA

'The original Mad Men are all dead. Ironically, they died from consuming the products they sold with such gusto. Their lungs went from the cigarettes they advertised – and smoked by the carton. Their livers melted from all the scotch, gin and vodka they made famous – and the three-martini lunches they enjoyed in the process . . .'

The original Mad Men are all dead.

Ironically, they died from consuming the products they sold with such gusto. Their lungs went from the cigarettes they advertised – and smoked by the carton. Their livers melted from all the scotch, gin and vodka they made famous – and the three-martini lunches they enjoyed in the process.

I wrote *From Those Wonderful Folks Who Brought You Pearl Harbor* in 1970. What you are about to read is a candid, inside look at a wild period in business, a new era of Mad Men that we will never again see.

I came into the advertising business in 1952 at the age of sixteen, as a delivery boy for a stuffy, old-line advertising agency named Ruthrauff & Ryan, which could have served as the setting for the *Mad Men* television series without moving a desk. Needless to say, it was a difficult business to break into, especially for a teenager with a limited education.

In 1956, I took my portfolio of sample creative work to J. Walter Thompson, the world's largest advertising agency. They had a position open for a junior writer of sales promotion on the Ford Truck account. At that time Ford was J. Walter Thompson's largest account.

The copy chief on the account looked at my work and said, 'This is very good, but I can't suggest you for the job.'

'Why?' I asked.

His answer was delivered with a nervous smile. 'Because this is Ford and they don't want your kind working on their business.'

It took me years to figure out what 'your kind' meant.

Advertising agencies in those days were broken down among ethnic lines. The Mad Men flourished in large

Protestant ad agencies like J. Walter Thompson and N.W. Ayer, BBDO and Ted Bates. These agencies monopolized all the large advertising accounts (cars, food, cigarettes, soft drinks, beer). The other, smaller accounts (dress manufacturers, shoes, underwear, small retail stores) were regulated to tiny, 'Jewish' ad agencies. By 1950 only one agency whose founders were Jewish had managed to win packaged goods, cigarette, liquor and car accounts. They did so by naming their agency after the color of the walls in their office, and by not using their Jewish names on their masthead – thus Grey Advertising was born.

Then, in the mid-1950s, a 'Jewish' advertising agency broke through the ethnic barrier. Doyle Dane Bernbach's campaign for advertisers like Volkswagen ('Think Small', 'Lemon') and Levy's Bread ('You don't have to be Jewish to love Levy's') changed the advertising business. Doyle Dane Bernbach made distinctive advertising that had 'attitude' and respected the consumer's intelligence. They sold products with ads that had humor, bold language and layouts with sharp, clean and stylish design. It opened the door for a totally new kind of Mad Man.

By 1961, when I got my first copywriting job, 'my kind' were suddenly in demand. The creative revolution had begun. Advertising had turned into a business dominated by young, funny, Jewish copywriters and tough, sometimes violent, Greek and Italian art directors.

The original Mad Men did not give up without a fight.

I once attended an advertising conference held at the Greenbrier Hotel in 1968. The dean of the original Mad Men, the great David Ogilvy, was the keynote speaker. The subject of his speech was the new creative revolution in advertising. Ogilvy knew his audience was mostly made up of desperate men who were trapped in agencies that were losing accounts to young, upstart, ethnic agencies. Ogilvy lashed out and declared, 'I say the lunatics have taken over the asylum!'

The audience rose and gave that fighting line a standing ovation. I stood up and was clapping as loudly as the next man when I suddenly thought to myself, *What are you clapping about – he's talking about you.*

It was a wonderful asylum. We were wild. We made the antics depicted on every episode of *Mad Men* look like *Rebecca of Sunnybrook Farm.* Our little agency was permanently filled with the sweet smell of burning cannabis. Life was easy was back in the days before human resource departments controlled business and someone decided we all should be politically correct. Everyone smoked (I had a four-pack-a-day habit). Everyone drank martinis (I had many a three-martini lunch), and everyone screwed around.

In the business world of the 1950s and early 60s, sex was a forbidden subject – everyone did it and no one talked about it. But by 1965 the sexual revolution was on, and the advertising business went wild. I encouraged it at my agency because nothing got creative people to come in early and leave late better than the prospect of sexual adventure.

In 1967, when I opened my ad agency, Jerry Della Femina & Partners, a group of us started an Agency Sex Contest. For more than twenty-five years, one week at the end of every year was devoted to *Animal House*-like antics. This was, until today, the best-kept secret in advertising. Thousands of people took part in the Agency Sex Contest.

The contest had everyone in the agency voting anonymously on paper ballots for the three people they most wanted to go to bed with. They were also asked to vote on the person of the same sex they would consider going to bed with. And, of course, there was the *ménage a trois* category, in which they selected the two other people they wanted to go to bed with. Sometimes as many as 300 votes were cast.

For one week the walls of the agency were covered with posters made by people who were campaigning for themselves. One very shy girl in Accounting got into the spirit of the contest, Xeroxed her breasts and hung pictures of them on the walls. Another young account executive had as her slogan: VOTE FOR AMANDA [not her real name]. LIKE BLOOMINGDALE'S, I'M OPEN AFTER 9 EVERY NIGHT.

One very attractive female executive had a sexy picture of herself that she sneaked into the agency's men's room, and put up on the wall that a man would be facing. The caption under her provocative photo read, CAN I HELP YOU WITH THAT? This almost caused a disaster when a rather priggish client called and said he was on his way to visit the agency. In the hour before he arrived, we feverishly took down every campaign ad. Then, in the course of the meeting, the man excused himself to go to the men's room. After a few minutes I let out a scream. We had forgotten to take the campaign posters off men's bathroom wall. The client returned ashen-faced. He never said a word about the signs but he kept shaking his head. I would walk out of the meeting every five minutes just to giggle and then come back looking like the proper head of a major advertising agency.

Voting was on the up and up. One year I had our accounting firm tally up the ballots. You never saw so many accountants looking so amused and animated in your life.

First prize for the winning couple (even if they hadn't voted for each other) was a weekend at the Plaza Hotel, paid for by my agency. Second prize was a night at the Plaza. Third prize was a night uninterrupted on the couch in my office. Winners of the *ménage a trois* got dinner for three at the Four Seasons Restaurant. Winners of the gay and lesbian part of the contest won a $100 gift certificate to The Pleasure Chest – a store in Greenwich Village that sold sex toys.

The results were announced at a party where as many as 300 of us would lock ourselves in a giant Mexican restaurant. At one party, I was concerned that the entire agency had imbibed too much cannabis and too many margaritas, and that the party was getting dangerously out of hand. When one older executive passed out, his head went into the plate of food in front of him. The woman next to him shouted, 'He's OK, the guacamole broke his fall.' A pretty, young, Asian woman, whom I'd never heard say a single word, jumped up on a table and started stripping and dancing with wild abandon, and accidentally kicked one of my art directors in the head. I rushed to the restaurant's manager and asked him to tell his waiters to cut down on the drinks. He smiled at me and said, 'Señor, it's too late. My waiters are all stoned and they are in the middle of the party.'

Was it sophomoric? You bet.

Was it politically incorrect? You bet.

Will you be seeing it in future shows of *Mad Men*? You bet.

By 1972 we were one of the fastest growing advertising agencies in the world. That's the year I decided to buy a smallish British agency called Saatchi & Saatchi. Why not? My book had been a best-seller, I was riding high and I decided I had to do something to tone down my image. Too many people saw me as being a wild man, and the larger, packaged-goods advertising accounts like Procter & Gamble and Lever Brothers would not deal with a wild man. I'd opened an office in Los Angeles – but no one ever changed his or her image at the Beverly Hills Hotel. So I looked to the UK for respectability.

I sent the president of my advertising agency, Jim Travis, to scout agencies in London. He came back and said the picking were slim. There was one agency – Collett, Dickson & Pearce – that was turning out great work, but they gave no indication that they wanted to be purchased. Our best chance was Saatchi & Saatchi, and they had expressed some interest in being acquired. I confess I had never heard of Saatchi & Saatchi, but I jumped onto a plane and went to London to make the deal.

I was greeted at the door of Saatchi & Saatchi like a conquering hero. 'We've all read your book,' someone said. 'We loved it,' someone else said. This was followed by fifteen minutes of small talk that frankly turned my incredibly swollen head. Compliment after compliment after compliment. *They're very nice*, I thought. I still remember admiring the large poster on their wall for Great Britain's Health Education Council (HEC) that featured a distinctly large-bellied man with the caption, 'Would you be more careful if it was you that got pregnant?' A great ad. *This, I thought, will be a good deal for both of our companies.*

Fifteen minutes later, with the small talk out of the way, I remember thinking, *They're smart*. More talk, more talk on how we might get together. I remember thinking, *They're very smart*.

Another fifteen minutes went by, as they told me how I might buy them and proposed a complicated reverse takeover. That's when it hit me. *Oh my God. They're smarter than I am. I've got to get out of here while I still have an ad agency.* I remember backing out the door, and heaving a sigh of relief as I stumbled out into the daylight. It was a close call – a street-smart Mad Man from America had just escaped the clutches of a couple of even smarter Mad Men from the UK.

A few months after my meeting with Saatchi & Saatchi, John O'Conner, a reporter friend from *Advertising Age*, called and said, 'Got some news for you. Compton Advertising just bought Saatchi & Saatchi.'

Now if there was an advertising agency that would have epitomized *Mad Men* it was Compton Advertising. Their former copy chief/president, Milton Gossett, could have been a double for Don Draper. 'Oh,' I said. 'Saatchi owns Compton.'

'No,' he said, 'You didn't hear me. Compton owns Saatchi.'

'Well,' I said, 'Saatchi will eventually own Compton.'

'You're out of your mind' was O'Conner's answer. I hung up the phone after making a small bet with O'Conner that the minnow from the UK would swallow the whale from the US. A few months later, in a reverse takeover, Saatchi & Saatchi owned Compton and proceeded to take over the advertising world.

In 1986 I bowed to the British buying spree and sold my agency, Della Femina McNamee, to a British company called White Collins Rutherford & Scott. It was sort of a mini reverse takeover on my part, because my agency took over all the agencies that White Collins Rutherford & Scott had acquired in the US.

Everyone who watches *Mad Men* asks me the same question: Has the advertising business changed?

Yes, dramatically.

To paraphrase Mr. Ogilvy's comment in 1968, the lunatics

are back in their cells, dead or retired. The internet is king. Newspapers are dead or dying. Magazines are shrinking every day. Ad budgets are being cut. The bottom line is now the only line in advertising. Copy has taken a back seat to design, and television advertising is shrinking because every client is looking for digital solutions. They want more and more, and want it to cost less and less. A few nineteen-year-old students from the School of Visual Arts in New York can design and produce a brilliant campaign in a few hours that once would have taken weeks of late-night creative work by fifty people to produce.

Me? I'm still in the business, running an ad agency called Della Femina Rothschild Jeary & Partners. I'm as in love with the business as when I was a sixteen-year-old mail boy at Ruthrauff & Ryan.

Once a Mad Man, always a Mad Man.

CHAPTER ONE
NAZIS DON'T TAKE AWAY ACCOUNTS

'The image of advertising still hangs in. The movie *Blow-Up* is a good example. Here's this scrawny English photographer – a fashion photographer – and in one scene these two chicks literally attack him on his purple no-seam backdrop. Thousands of people watch this photographer jumping from one chick to the next and they think, Wow! Imagine what goes on in advertising if this is what happens to a photographer. So another whole batch of people decides to quit delivering milk or whatever the hell they were doing and they've made up their minds to get into advertising . . .'

Most people think advertising is Tony Randall. In fact, they think this business is made up of 90,000 Tony Randalls. Guys all very suave, all very Tony Randall. They've been fed the idea from Hollywood that an advertising man is a slick, sharp guy. The people know zip about advertising.

In the 1930s, everybody figured Adolphe Menjou was your typical advertising man. They dumped Adolphe Menjou by 1940 and then we had Melvyn Douglas. Remember him? There was a difference between Menjou and Douglas. Menjou was superficial; he knew nothing about it. Douglas knew nothing about it, and didn't care either. Sometimes Menjou looked like he might be worried about losing a big account. But Douglas, like he spent most of his time in those movies screwing Rosalind Russell. So he couldn't care less about losing the account. All of those movies were the same. Scene one, you pan up a New York skyscraper with some of that hokey New York music, then the camera moves into the elevator of the building. Douglas walks into the building, the elevator starter says, 'Good morning, Mr. Suave,' and the elevator door slams shut. Next shot you see the elevator floor dial moving up to 18. Douglas gets off the elevator, walks through the office, and the next thing you know he's screwing somebody. It's strange, really crazy. That's what advertising was like in the movies. And Douglas never had real problems, but he was in advertising – he was the symbol of the guy who was in advertising.

Clark Gable. A beautiful guy. Played the hero in *The Hucksters*, the guy who bails out the tough soap account – although the book was modeled after George Washington Hill of the American Tobacco Company.

The Hucksters must have pulled in a lot of guys off the street into advertising. There was the image. Gable's main concern was getting laid every hour on the Super Chief between Chicago and the Coast. The movie had something going for it.

Then the image changed to Randall. He's slick and suave. Underneath, he's like a shell. He's terrible. Down deep Randall is really a very shallow guy. The real business is much closer to Wally Cox because Cox, unlike Randall, shows fear. Cox is real; you see him. I've dealt with guys like Cox.

I know a guy at a very large agency – I'll call him Jim – who's got courage. Pilot, World War II. He couldn't fly in America in 1940 because he was only seventeen years old so he went and joined the Royal Canadian Air Force. Bright, and a lot of courage. He flew in the Battle of Britain, the whole thing. Gets out of the service and doesn't know what to do. He's still a kid because he enlisted when he was eighteen. Anyhow, Jim goes to work for a small advertising agency because it seems like a glamorous thing to do. He's still courageous and bright, then. And as he grows older he gets scared that he might lose his salary, his expense account. The higher he goes, the more frightened he gets. The guy now is a frightened little man, and today he's only someplace in his forties.

I once asked him what happened between the time that he was shooting down planes and now, when he is a terrified account executive. He looked at me and said, 'Well, for one thing, the Nazis never tried to take away one of my accounts.'

The average person who sits and watches Tony Randall perform ought to be around a large, bad agency when the big account is pulled out. Nobody cries the first day. What happens is an announcement comes around that says, 'We regret to announce . . .' The next thing that happens is that the president of the agency says, 'Screw them. They were never any good in the first place.' That's the unofficial attitude. They might even break out the drinks and everybody is talking: 'We're better off without them. We never needed them and now we're really going to pull in the new business.' It's a very interesting thing to watch. As the account guys are talking they start to break off into little groups. Immediate bravado. 'Hey, we got rid of those sons of bitches. I'll never have to put up with that bastard again. And his wife is a drunk.' Then they break off into even smaller groups. On that first day, excitement. 'We lost it!' And the next day, death. The calls go out, guys get out their address books and start calling anyone they ever met in business. The second day they start calling Judy Wald, the lady who runs one of the largest personnel agencies in the business. 'Judy,' they say, 'I'd like to bring my book over.' Guys start leaving the office with suspicious-looking big packages under their arms. Those packages, it's their portfolio, their work, anything that they could put together that is going to get them a job. Everybody immediately assumes he's going to lose his job.

The top, the very top management very wisely stakes out a claim on an account not already in the house. Let's take a hypothetical example – let's say your agency loses Texaco Gas. Suddenly an executive vice-president says, 'I went to school with a guy from Sinclair, and they must be tired of those folks over at Cunningham and Walsh. I'm going to give old Jack a call. Maybe we can have a few drinks. I think I can line up something with Sinclair.'

Not to be outdone, another vice-president says, 'I have a cat over at Esso. Forget about your guy at Sinclair. My guy at Esso, like we not only went to school together, we fought in the Army together. Esso is unhappy with their agency. My friend has told me so many times. I think we really could work out something with Esso.'

Each biggie in the agency picks a major company that he's going to shoot for. This is the way they express their fear. They all talk about a big piece of business that they could bring into the house. Nothing ever happens, but that doesn't matter. They try. They honestly believe that they can do it. What beautiful calls they make. The executive vice-president calls his pal Jack, who may or may not remember who this guy is, and he says, 'Hi, Jack, you see we've just been screwed by Texaco. What do you say we get together and have a drink?' He has his drink with pal Jack, and then he goes back to his agency and at a management meeting he says, 'When I said to Jack that we lost the account, he smiled at me. I *know* that smile. I *know* the way he smiled at me – he was trying to tell me, "I can't give it to you now, baby, but in six months it's yours." I have heard those exact words. There's a slight variation on it. 'When he said no, he said no in such a way that he was opening a door for us – he really was saying that in six months it's ours. We've got it.' That's how top management lies to itself and how these guys lie to each other. After a while they forget about it. They're out pitching new business, holding meetings, fooling around with the creative departments, and they forget all about pal Jack and how old school buddy Jack was going to give them Esso, or Sinclair, or Shell, or whatever the hell it was they were pitching. The biggies keep occupied. They *must* keep busy. As for the little people, they've already been screwed by the biggies. They haven't got a chance. They've been fired.

The image of advertising still hangs in. The movie *Blow-Up* is a good example. Here's this scrawny English photographer – a fashion photographer – and in one scene these two chicks literally attack him on his purple no-seam backdrop.

Thousands of people watch this photographer jumping from one chick to the next and they think, Wow! Imagine what goes on in advertising if this is what happens to a photographer. So another whole batch of people decides to quit delivering milk or whatever the hell they were doing and they've made up their minds to get into advertising.

Those who don't go into the business talk about it. You meet them at cocktail parties and they say to you, 'Do you put the captions under the pictures or do you take the pictures?' That's the difference to them between an art director and a copywriter. A copywriter puts the captions under the pictures. As far as these people are concerned, you're only playing around. They think you walk around during the day freaked out on acid or hash, and in between trips you're carrying on with the women.

A friend I grew up with in Brooklyn – he's a fireman today – once said to me, 'Boy, day in day out – models coming out of your ears. You must be killing yourself. I've been up to your office and I've seen the girls with the miniskirts. I mean, there really must be a lot of fooling around in that business. Can I come up and see? I just want to walk around and see.' He wants to be part of it. He figures the models must be making it with everyone, and then, of course, you're doing commercials, and that means actresses. As far as he's concerned, I'm in Hollywood and the whole world is one big casting couch.

This rumored playing around is so exaggerated. The average model is, first of all, so dumb that nobody even wants to approach her. And neurotic! This is the most neurotic group of people that you could ever want to be with. The average model is so uptight that she's impossible. You have to remember one thing about models: they live on their looks, and their only job is to look beautiful. Yet, five times a day, they go to an agency like Ted Bates or J. Walter Thompson and sit around in a room with fifteen other girls who look just as beautiful. It's like a meat market. The art director stands there and says, 'O.K., girls, stand up. Turn around. Say "Duz does it," with a French accent.' So the girls walk around, mumble 'Duz does it' with a French accent – or without a French accent, it doesn't matter – and at the end of the session the art director says, 'O.K. You, over there, you can stay. Thanks for coming by, everybody.'

I once interviewed fifteen models for a feminine-hygiene spray which we handle, and one model got the job. Fourteen were rejected. Those models go from our rejection to another rejection to another rejection to a point where they're going out of their skulls. How many times can you be rejected a day?

So the average model is so crazy that most guys wouldn't want to go near her. Besides, the only person in an agency who comes in contact with models is the art director, or maybe the account executive. The models are really not concerned with the art directors anyway, because it's a one-shot job and there just can't be a casting-couch situation. The art director hires the model for one commercial and he may never see her again.

The only people who wind up sleeping with models are photographers. And photographers are monkeys. I mean, they're *really* monkeys. You know, most photographers are very short and have very long arms. I guess the long arms come from carrying those bags around – that's a lot of equipment they haul around. Some photographers' arms scrape the ground, they're so long. The funny bit is that they make out as far as models are concerned. I may be projecting now, which is what my fireman friend is doing. The fireman's decided that I'm making it with every model in town and I've decided that the photographers are the ones who are really making it with the models.

If there's little glamour in advertising with adult models, there's even less for kid models. You ought to see kid models. Kid models practically eat the rug, they're so crazy. They're out of their minds. And the mothers are insane, too.

When I was working at the Daniel & Charles agency, we had to do a commercial for a children's toy called Colorforms. Because we couldn't afford to go and do the commercial on location, we had to settle for Central Park in the dead of winter. We got the kids into polo shirts and short pants and went out to the park. It must have been like maybe ten or fifteen degrees above zero and there was snow all over the place. We managed to shovel off one patch where the kids were going to play with the toy. The kids were turning blue and screaming; the mothers were screaming at the kids because they didn't want the kids to blow the job. It was terrible.

Once an agency was shooting a commercial on Fire Island, and there was the usual pack of people at the shooting – the kid model, the kid model's mother who was hanging on to the agency producer's ear, the director, the assistant director, prop men, grips, cameramen, script people, agency people, account people, the usual tremendous mob. Anyhow, they shoot the commercial, and it comes off okay and everybody packs up and starts walking to the dock to get the next ferry back to New York. The mother is still putting on the producer, telling him what a great actor her kid is; the cameraman is telling the director what a terrific job of camera work the commercial is; the copywriter is telling the account man what a great script he wrote – the usual nonsense from everyone concerned. Everybody gets to the ferry and they're starting to get on when somebody turns around – and it wasn't the mother, either – and says, 'Hey, where's the kid?' Well, everyone starts looking high and low for the kid and it turns out they had left the kid back on the beach. Just left him there, playing in the sand.

When I was working at Bates, I happened to be walking through the reception area one day when suddenly I found myself surrounded by little Chinese boys. I mean, the place was jammed with them. There must have been at least fifty Chinese mothers there too. Now the Chinese are a very stable group; they're probably the sanest group of people in New York. Yet there were enough crazy Chinese mothers to fill up the halls of Bates with these little Chinese kids, all looking for their job. Again, one Chinese kid is needed – and think of the rejections. Fifty Chinese kids could start a revolution if they got rejected enough.

You've got to go crazy to be a model. During one of the periods when I was out of work I shot a commercial on spec using my own kid because I couldn't afford to hire a kid model. As we walked out, I noticed my kid was high. She was up. She was so spaced out that she wasn't a kid any more. She was way out of it almost as if she was on pot. She couldn't talk, she was breathing heavily. It's a crazy experience for a kid to have to do this. It gives them the idea that they're better than normal people because they're in an ad.

When I was working for Fuller & Smith & Ross, I happened to be on the agency basketball team. One night our team had a game scheduled with a group of male models. Invariably the word is out that all male models are fags. It's not true that all of them are, but quite a few of them are a little too cute for words.

Anyhow, here come the male models, and five of the most

beautiful guys in the world come out and run across the floor. We were staring at them, that's how beautiful they were. And, like we figured, you know – male models – we're going to kill them. We forgot one thing: quite a few of the male models are ex-jocks out of colleges. It was a great scene. The game gets started and pretty soon I get a break and start dribbling toward their basket. I'm all alone, or I thought I was alone. I'm going up for a lay-up, and as I go up one of these guys – he was six foot four, so help me – one of these beautiful, beautiful guys comes down on me with his elbow and catches me across the top of the nose. I fell to the floor and I couldn't see for a second, the pain was so unbelievable. Blood was gushing out of my nose, all over me, the floor, everything. As I was bouncing around on the floor I remember I was shouting, 'My nose, my nose!' And this beautiful guy just looks down at me and says, 'You call *that* a nose?' It was so funny that I was laughing and bleeding at the same time.

I could give you all the disclaimers in the world, but people are still going to look enviously at the advertising business. I just don't understand it. In the average insurance office there must be a lot of fooling around going on, and yet the average insurance office isn't as glamorous as the advertising business supposedly is. Many years ago when I was flat broke and selling toys in Macy's and then bathrobes in Gimbel's basement, I used to think about all the jazz in the advertising business. Just recently I heard about a book called *Seventh Avenue*, in which everybody in the garment business was chasing to beat the band. I tell you, when I was sitting there in Gimbel's basement, it didn't seem so glamorous to me. There are guys who are screwing around in every business. I'm sure there are plenty of carpenters doing things besides putting up bookshelves. And milkmen too. There's just this crazy glamor to advertising, and we can't shake it.

* * *

Take booze. At the very large, established agencies there's no casual boozing during the day. Clark Gable was always knocking down a quickie before a meeting. At Bates, there's no liquor for the troops. You just don't drink if you're a troop. You may drink at Bates if you're one of the very, very biggies, but then only in your office. Whenever an agency picks up an account somebody might be a sport and buy some New York State champagne. At J. Walter Thompson, forget it. They've barely accepted the fact that such a thing as liquor exists. For years, Thompson wouldn't even take a liquor account because their chairman was anti-booze. The surest way to be fired at Thompson in those days was to show up bagged.

Go through all the larger agencies and there's very little drinking going on. Oh, a guy might drink at lunch, and there's always a handful of guys at an agency with what everyone calls 'a problem.' But there's always a few guys at a brokerage house with the same problem.

When I worked at Fuller & Smith & Ross seven years ago there was an account executive who was quite a boozer. You knew that if you wanted to talk to him you talked to him like at eleven in the morning because at 3:00 p.m. you're talking but the guy isn't there – he's out of it. He's drunk, and he's doing some pretty strange things. Those guys who do booze – the hard core of agency drinkers – they're all bagged by noon. The only thing you have to remember when you've got business to do with them is be sure and get to them before lunch.

At our agency at the end of the day we haul out the booze, get a bucket of ice, and whoever wants a drink takes one. At the newer and looser agencies around town they do a little boozing. No one's uncomfortable about my seeing them drink, because they've seen me drink. No one feels uncomfortable about opening a bottle at our agency. An account executive can run over and grab a bottle here without me saying, 'Boy, is he having a drinking problem. We're going to have to watch him closely.' There's probably more drinking done at our agency than at most other agencies in New York.

There are always a couple of guys who spur the drinking on. When I worked at Delehanty, Kurnit & Geller, I was one of the guys who did the spurring. My thing was I had to steal Shep Kurnit's booze. He was the president, and I had to get at his stuff. For a period of six months, whenever Shep would have a client in, he would open his liquor cabinet – which he kept locked – and reach in for his booze and it was gone. He knew I was taking it. The whole agency would wait for me to steal it – that was the scene. Finally he came up to me one day and he said, 'Jerry, look, I won't say anything but you've got to tell me how you get into the liquor cabinet. I'll buy it for you, but you just have to tell me how you get into a locked liquor cabinet.'

Shep had a letter opener on his desk, given to him by the One Hundred Million Club, a direct-mail organization. I took the letter opener and said, 'Watch. I'm going to open the cabinet faster than you do with a key.' I shoved the letter opener into the cabinet and popped the lock without any trouble. The cabinet door swung open. Shep looked at me and said, 'O.K. I'll leave the cabinet open, but don't screw around with my letter opener.' Shep is such a beautiful person.

Sometimes people at agencies don't actually booze in their offices; instead, they hang out at certain bars. For instance, the Doyle, Dane people hang out at the Teheran, which is a bar over on Forty-fourth Street. It's their bar, Big carrying-on bar, big coming-and-going bar. Friday nights are the heavy nights at the Teheran. Guys who left Doyle, Dane fifteen years ago find their way back to the Teheran on Friday nights. The Delehanty people used to hang out a lot at the Mount D'Or, over on East Forty-sixth, and at P.J. Clarke's.

At the swinging agencies – Wells, Rich; Doyle, Dane; Delehanty; Carl Ally, Papert, Koenig, Lois; Lois, Holland, Callaway; Smith/Greenland; Daniel & Charles; Spade & Archer – all of them are more casual, looser, more fun. Even the dress is a lot different. I've got a twenty-two-year-old art director who wears Uncle Sam pants, see-through shirts, and God knows what else. But he's good, and as long as he's good he can work naked for all I care. One day at Ted Bates, a girl wore a pair of culottes to the office. She really was great-looking, a beautiful chick. The next day there was a memo saying, you know, bug off, no more of this culotte jazz, this is an office of business. All of the giant agencies try to maintain their offices as a place that you would want to put your money into. It's got to be very banklike, and very sleepy.

When I say things are looser, the average person immediately makes rampant orgies out of that statement. Everybody knows the story about the wild Christmas party they supposedly had at Young & Rubicam years ago. According to one version, the wife of the president of the agency walked into one of the offices and found a copywriter making it with his secretary. Well, I don't believe it. But everybody on Madison Avenue swears it's true. When I was working at Fuller & Smith & Ross it supposedly took place at Fuller & Smith & Ross. It's probably apocryphal. I just don't think that that many guys can get caught in the saddle. Another one of those stories: A guy used to go to work at six in the morning and make it with a chick on the conference-room table. Don't believe it for a minute.

Take the president of one agency where I once worked. This guy always thought that we were making it in his office. He was very, very shook about that. Well, here's a case of a guy who's in advertising but he's also living this vicarious life. He goes back to Darien every night, but he would like to feel that there is a lot of screwing going on in the business because it makes him feel happy to think that his boys are out there carrying on. He likes the idea of having a bunch of Peck's bad boys working for him. He doesn't do any of this carrying on, but he likes to talk about his crazies when he's out at some party in Connecticut. It's nice for him to say to himself as he rides home on the train: Gee, there's a lot of screwing going on in my agency – why, right this second I'll bet they're making it on my couch. When he comes in the next day and finds a girl's bobby pin on his couch he immediately decides that they were making it the night before.

A couple of summers ago we started playing a few games of strip poker in our office. Nothing serious, just for a few laughs. I was walking through the hall one day and this nice girl came running out of a guy's office buttoning her blouse. I looked into the office and there was this guy, with a deck of cards in his hand and a smile on his face. He had said to her, 'Do you want to play strip poker?' She said, sure, why not, and she lost her blouse. So the mood in the office that week was sort of strip-poker-oriented. But nothing more serious than that.

A lot of people have accused the younger creative people in advertising of being a bunch of potheads. Let me say a few words about grass. As I walk around New York City, it seems to me that a good 50 percent of the population under the age of thirty looks like it's either stoned, about to get stoned, or coming down from a high. None of the kids drink any more. All of the drinking at our agency is done by those of us who are over thirty. Throughout advertising, you've got a hell of a lot of young kids working who laugh at anyone who drinks. I guess you'd find that hundreds of the younger people have tried grass at one time or another – in advertising and out of it.

An art director I know had a freelance assignment to do some work for an avant-garde publisher down in the Village. While he's sitting in their offices the other day, a secretary says, 'Would you like a smoke?' He says innocently, 'Sure.' And the chick hauls out the whole business, complete with a water cooler or hookah or whatever the hell they call those things. So he fired up. Little does he know that the cops have been keeping binoculars trained on this publisher for quite some time, and just as he and the chick are about to go up, here come the cops. He got busted, which I guess goes to show you that you shouldn't accept a smoke from a stranger.

Despite all the talk about romance, boozing, and carrying on, the advertising business is not what you think it is. Crazy? Yes. Romantic and glamorous? Not one bit. The wild stuff, I'm afraid, is very much overrated.

CHAPTER TWO

WHO KILLED SPEEDY ALKA-SELTZER?

'Good advertising gets exposure. People talk about it, notice it, think about it. The client is standing up there waiting at the train station for the New Haven to take him into New York and he's dying to be stopped by his buddies. He is dying for them to compliment him on his new campaign. Everyone wants to be praised. "Boy, you've got a hell of an ad there." That's what the client wants to hear. Plus the cash register . . .'

In the beginning, there was Volkswagen. That's the first campaign which everyone can trace back and say, 'This is where the changeover began.' That was the day when the new advertising agency was really born, and it all started with Doyle, Dane, Bernbach. They began as an agency around 1949 and they were known in the business as a good agency, but no one really got to see what they were doing until Volkswagen came around.

Volkswagen was being handled in the United States by Fuller & Smith & Ross. Doyle, Dane took the account over around 1959. One of the first ads to come out for Volkswagen was the first ad that anyone can remember when the new agency style really came through with an entirely different look. That ad simply said, 'Lemon.' The copy for 'Lemon' said once in a while we turn out a car that's a lemon, in which case we get rid of it. We don't sell them. And we are careful as hell with our cars, we test them before we sell them, so the chances are you'll never get one of our lemons.

For the first time in history an advertiser said that he was capable, on rare occasions, of turning out an inferior product. An advertiser was saying that all wasn't sweetness in life, that everything wasn't fantastic in the world of business, and people took to it immediately. Volkswagen became a successful campaign, and an overwhelmingly successful product.

No one had ever called his product a lemon before. By today's standards, of course, this is pretty ordinary stuff. It was the first time anyone really took a realistic approach to advertising. It was the first time the advertiser ever talked to the consumer as though he was a grownup instead of a baby.

Before 'Lemon,' they ran an ad that said, 'Think Small.' Now the average American car buyer, who has been raised on chrome and plastic and tailfins all his life, looks at that ad and starts to think small. The Detroit reaction to all this was: It will never do. What is this, calling your product a lemon? It was the equivalent of a politician saying, 'I'm not going to keep all my promises. I'm going to lie on occasion.' It was the first time anyone ever told the truth in print. And the reaction was immediate – people started talking about Volkswagen advertising.

The Volkswagen ads didn't make a big fetish of the company's name. They kept their name down in a very small logotype at the bottom of the ad. It was handled in such a way that somebody was talking directly to the consumer in a language which the consumer was dying to hear. It was a tremendous success. 'Lemon,' 'Think Small,' all of them not only built up Volkswagen but led directly to the advertising we have today.

Detroit, of course, not only ignored the advertising – they ignored the message of the small car, too. After Volkswagen came Renault and Volvo and Peugeot and dozens of others. Detroit figured what this country still needs is a large boat that you can't park and falls apart in three years. First Detroit brought out the compacts, like the Corvair and the Falcon. These really weren't small cars and the public realized it by not buying them in droves. The compacts were cheap imitations of what the foreign small cars were all about. In 1964 Detroit finally admitted there might be something to this small-car stuff, and Ford produced the Mustang. Mustang was still selling very strong in 1969. Only fifteen years after Volkswagen.

Advertising still downgrades the consumer's intelligence because the people who are doing the ads are often as stupid as the people they think they're talking to. The advertising industry is full of thickheaded guys. Just recently a creative director of an old-line agency was quoted in one of the trade papers as saying that this direct method of talking to people won't work. This guy says that Doyle, Dane, Bernbach is a passing fad; it's going to go away and quit bothering him someday.

Some passing fad! They passed his agency five years ago. His agency was doing about $125 million a year ago. Who knows what Doyle, Dane are doing? They pick up business so fast you can't even keep up with it. They're billing maybe $255 million and they're booming. They just don't stop.

Anything Doyle, Dane touches turns to gold – with the exception of beer. They did a great job with the Polaroid Land Camera. If you want to say that anyone could have done a terrific job with Polaroid, because the product is so unique, O.K., let's not waste time on Polaroid. Take Levy's Rye Bread. They get Levy's bread and maybe an ad budget of $100,000 and all of a sudden pictures of Indians are appearing all over town saying, 'You Don't Have to Be Jewish to Enjoy Levy's Rye.' As far as I'm concerned, all rye bread tastes the same, but look what Doyle, Dane did for it. What happens is a guy at General Foods looks at all those Indians and Chinese and pictures of Godfrey Cambridge pushing Levy's and he says, 'What the hell are we doing with the agency we have? Look at what these guys are doing for $100,000.' The next thing you know, Doyle, Dane gets a piece of General Foods. They start doing great work for General Foods and the guy over at Kraft says, 'Look at this. For years we've been hanging around doing nothing. Let's get somebody like these guys and quit getting killed by General Foods.' The cry is going out all over town, 'Give me a Doyle, Dane agency, give me a Doyle, Dane ad.'

Good advertising gets exposure. People talk about it, notice it, think about it. The client is standing up there waiting at the train station for the New Haven to take him into New York and he's dying to be stopped by his buddies. He is dying for them to compliment him on his new campaign. Everyone wants to be praised. 'Boy, you've got a hell of an ad there.' That's what the client wants to hear. Plus the cash register. He loves it when his friends say, 'You people are really doing a job.' He wants that desperately. There's a myth that the client is not interested in awards. Nonsense. Clients love awards because they love recognition just as much as agencies do. They want their accounts to win as many awards as possible.

Doyle, Dane's advertising has that feeling that the consumer is bright enough to understand what the advertising is saying, that the consumer isn't a lunkhead who has to be treated like a twelve-year-old. People are more sophisticated today. It's not just because of television, although that's part of it. It's a matter that I'm brighter than my father, and my son is going to be brighter than I am. I don't understand what the new math is, but my kids will; they're going to be way ahead of me. They're much sharper, they know exactly what's going on in the world. The average consumer, you know, doesn't buy the junky advertising any more. He doesn't buy a line like Luckies tasting milder. He doesn't believe the male model decked out in a fruity sailor suit claiming that the cigarette he's smoking has that 'lusty' taste. It's archaic. Guys who do this sort of advertising may be twenty years behind their time. In a sense, even Doyle, Dane may be behind its time. We still haven't really learned to communicate with the consumer to a point where he can understand us all of the time. I know this is going to sound crazy, but I sometimes don't understand why we can't talk in commercials and ads the way we *really* talk – well, there are Government agencies that stop us from talking the way we *really* talk so I suppose that ends that.

There's a magazine out right now called *Screw* and if you can pick up a copy at your local newsstand without getting arrested, it's worth a look. Quite honestly, they may be overboard on one side, and yet they're talking closer to the way people talk and think and feel than the *Saturday Evening Post* did when it folded. *Screw* has more of an appeal; it's closer to what the people are.

Doyle, Dane is as close as you can get to what people really are and what people really think. When you run an ad in New York City for El Al Airlines with a headline that says, 'My Son, the Pilot,' you are talking the language of the people. It's a beautifully written ad, supposedly done by a woman who is talking about her son, a pilot for El Al, and her son is going to really take care of you on the flight. In fact, he's even going to take care of your heartburn from all the horseradish.

I love the El Al ads. Once, when I was at Fuller & Smith & Ross, those ads got me into a bit of trouble. We had just picked up one of the Arab airlines as an account. All I know is that there were a lot of guys wearing funny white things on their heads. I was instructed by the people at Fuller & Smith to take down all the ads tacked up on the walls of my office and keep the place absolutely spotless for the big meeting. I took this as a personal insult. I called up a friend of mine who worked at Doyle, Dane; this guy had every El Al ad and poster they had ever done. I loaded my wall with those El Al posters.

When the guy walking the Arab through the office opened my office door he started to say, 'And this is Mr. Della Femina, one of our creative . . .' He took one look at the walls and turned the Arab completely around and ran out of there. Later on, he called me down to his office and said, 'Jerry, that was a terrible thing you did. If Abdul had seen those ads it would have been very embarrassing to him as well as to the agency and it could have cost us the account.' But they all smoothed it over and I kept my job.

To get back to Fuller & Smith when they had Volkswagen, it's interesting how an agency thinks of an account after it leaves and becomes a smash success. The attitude is, Gee, isn't it amazing that Volkswagen, which was run by lunkheads when they were at Fuller & Smith, went over to Doyle, Dane and became a very hip group of guys. Same management, same people. They're at Fuller & Smith and they're turning out crap. The next day they go to Doyle, Dane, Bernbach and they turn out great advertising. So how can you blame the management of Volkswagen?

Eastern Airlines was considered a terrible account in the industry when it was at Benton & Bowles in 1964. One day they went over to Young & Rubicam, which turned out great advertising for them. The management of Eastern didn't change overnight, the advertising did. Benson & Hedges was regarded as a dumb, rotten client at Benton & Bowles. They go over to Mary Wells in 1967 and she produces a great series of commercials showing people getting their extra-long Benson & Hedges stuck in elevator doors, and suddenly they turn out to be a bright, intelligent, great client.

There is no such thing as a bad client. But there is such a thing as bad advertising. This list is endless. Talon Zippers, when it was at McCann-Erickson in 1961, was considered to be one of the worst clients of our time. McCann would present campaigns, which were turned down by Talon. Talon hated the stuff McCann turned out and became very frustrated.

They couldn't get what they wanted, and naturally McCann, seeing all these rejected campaigns, thought that they were a lousy client. They weren't. So with the same advertising manager, the same management guys, they move over to Delehanty, Kurnit & Geller and suddenly Talon has great advertising.* I know for a fact that the Delehanty people don't regard Talon as a difficult client to deal with.

The blame isn't with the client. He'll take whatever is right for him. If he can't get it out of an agency that may be giving him garbage, he's stuck with that agency unless he makes a change. Braniff was at a little agency in Wisconsin when it moved over to Mary Wells, who then was working at Jack Tinker & Partners. The advertising improved right away. Take Alka-Seltzer. An agency called Wade had invented this little fairy, Speedy Alka-Seltzer, who could have passed for the son of Johnny from Philip Morris. They were trying to sell Alka-Seltzer with this little Speedy creep. Well, one day they moved the account over to Jack Tinker and the first thing Tinker did was to kill off Speedy. Or if they didn't kill him they had him arrested in the men's room of Grand Central Station on a charge of exposing himself. And they came up with a great campaign, 'Alka-Seltzer on the Rocks.' In 1969, Miles Laboratory pulled it out of Tinker and gave it to Doyle, Dane. I don't know why, but I do know that everybody concerned with the move praised Tinker for the superb job they had done.

Too many agency guys spend their time complaining about their clients. 'My client won't let me do anything. My

---

* Delehanty changed its name to D.K.G. late in 1969, but mostly I call it 'Delehanty' throughout the book – which is how the place continues to be known in the business.

client won't let me say anything.' But that same client goes over to another agency, which then turns out great work. It's a lot of crap. It's something these guys do as a defense to keep from going out of their minds, to keep them from understanding how incompetent they really are. How could a guy really say, 'Gee, you know, I'm an incompetent son of a bitch and that's why this work is turning out terrible.'

Good advertising comes from a good subject. Amend that: Good advertising is easier to come by when you have a good subject. Most airline advertising is terrific. In fact, almost all destination advertising is very good. They are talking about romantic spots throughout the world. I mean, who could fail when he's doing an ad for Tahiti? But have you seen a good ad lately for Korean Airways? You've got to admit their advertising isn't as good as, say, the advertising for Eastern where they used to show a kid jumping off a cliff into the water in Acapulco. You would really have to be a total incompetent to mess up an ad for Jamaica or actually a commercial for any city in this country. You can usually make something out of a city no matter which one it is. The airlines have produced commercials that make Chicago almost look like a palatable place. I mean, that's great advertising when you can turn Chicago into a city you'd want to spend more than three hours in. It gets a little tougher when you take a place like Detroit. Have you ever seen a good commercial for Detroit?

Destination advertising is the easiest stuff in the world to do. When I was at Delehanty we had the TAP (Portuguese) Airline account. You don't have to show a plane. You show the place you get to if you get on that plane. We turned out beautiful ads because Portugal is a great place to do ads for. We were very careful not to mention Salazar or the fact that if you did something wrong in Portugal you could have the world's first thirty-year vacation.

Advertising agencies can take an off-the-wall country like France and do a terrific job with it. But I'm always amused by the fact that some of the country's great liberals are in advertising and the ads these guys do for some of our better-known dictatorships in the world are terrific. They do great stuff for Spain, almost as good as Portugal. It's interesting how some people drop their political convictions when it comes to advertising. I know guys who would make you fly Nazi Airlines in a minute or get you to pack your voodoo kit for a little trip to Haiti.

The quality of most advertising really depends on what has to be said. You're writing ads on insurance, it's easy. It's great to do ads on the stock market. It's simple to do ads on a camera that gives you a picture sixty seconds after you shoot it. The big problem is the guy who has to do an ad for soap. Some poor son of a bitch is sitting in his office at Compton right this minute trying to figure out what to say about Ivory Soap that hasn't been said maybe twenty thousand times before. I mean, what do you say? Where do you go? No matter what you say, it's still soap.

This doesn't mean that your average soap ad or commercial couldn't be better. There are some guys who have given up a long time ago, but let me tell you there are reasons for a guy to struggle with a soap ad. It is very tough. If you're a guy doing an ad for Tide, what do you say? What do you do about Axion? Well, you go out and get Arthur Godfrey or Eddie Albert to say a few kind words about Axion, or whatever enzyme you're hustling.

We're having different problems with a product called Feminique. It's a vaginal-odor spray, plain and simple, but the magazines and the networks have decided in their minds that this country is not quite ready for the word vagina. We can't even say what our product is.

Feminine hygiene is going to be a big business for agencies. Our stuff, Feminique, is selling well. FDS is doing well. Johnson & Johnson came out with Vespré and it's doing well. The American businessman has discovered the vagina and like it's the next thing going. What happened is that the businessman ran out of parts of the body. We had headaches for a while but we took care of them. The armpit had its moment of glory, and the toes, with their athlete's foot, they had the spotlight, too. We went through wrinkles, we went through diets. Taking skin off, putting skin on. We went through the stomach with acid indigestion and we conquered hemorrhoids. So the businessman sat back and said, 'What's left?' And some smart guy said, 'The vagina.' We've now zeroed in on it. And this is just the beginning. Today the vagina, tomorrow the world. I mean, there are going to be all sorts of things for the vagina: vitamins, pep pills, flavored douches like Cupid's Quiver (raspberry, orange, jasmine, and champagne). If we can get by with a spray, we can sell anything new. And the spray is selling. In the first few months of 1969 the manufacturer of Feminique put something like $600,000 worth of it into the stores in test areas without one commercial ever being on the air. The maker of Feminique expects to break even if he has sales of $1,500,000 in the first year. But before the advertising even starts he's got $600,000 in the till. He's going to make it on reorders alone.

The first commercial we shot for Feminique was almost a disaster. We had a Swedish model walking through the woods in a scene very much like a take from the movie *Elvira Madigan*. The trouble was the girl couldn't speak English and then we discovered she couldn't even speak Swedish. And she was wooden. We shot the commercial up in a place called Sterling Forest, which is near Tuxedo Park, New York. When you're shooting commercials, people come around and ask you funny questions. A woman came up to me in the middle of the shooting and said, 'What are you doing?' I said, 'Oh, this is a commercial for Feminique.' Now she's never heard of Feminique, nothing had broken in the New York market, and yet she says, 'Oh, I use it all the time.'

I said, 'Really?' 'Oh, yes,' she said. 'And my husband uses it too.' I raised my eyebrows a little bit. I said, 'Do the children use it?' She said, 'Oh, no, no, we wouldn't let the children use it. Just my husband and me.' I politely thanked her and told her that the people at Feminique would be very happy to hear.

Some campaigns go bad for strange reasons. My partner, Ron Travisano, was working at Marschalk when they got a cake mix that was almost too good for the marketplace. All you had to do to make a cake was add water, but the product was going nowhere. They ran tests and then they ran more tests. They found out that the average housewife hated the product because if she couldn't do something physical in the making of the cake, she felt that she was being cheated. If all she had to do was add water, well, she felt that she really was nowhere as a homemaker and a cook. The product was just too slick.

So they pulled it back and did whatever you do to cake mixes and they fixed it so now to make a cake you had to break an egg. In the instructions they said if you break an egg into this mix and add water, you're going to have one hell of a cake. But without the egg the product is nothing. It worked. The very act of breaking an egg told the housewife that she was a cook again. The product worked, sold like hell. It was unbelievable.

Ron also was involved with a problem dealing with a first-aid cream, a Johnson & Johnson product. This stuff was a painless antiseptic for cuts, scratches, things like that. Now here's Johnson & Johnson, a hell of a good company, and they go and invent an antiseptic that doesn't drive you up the wall when you put it on. They send it out on a test and nobody buys the stuff the second time around. The company can't figure out what's wrong. They ran tests again and they discovered that people have to feel pain before they'll accept the fact that they're getting healed. They have to feel a burning sensation. And what's wrong with this stuff? It's obviously no good because when you put it on it doesn't burn. Forget that the cut is healing, there wasn't any burn.

So the guys at Johnson & Johnson who broke their backs to figure out this marvelous stuff put a little alcohol back into the cream for no other reason than to give the stuff a little wallop. I figure the research scientists really wondered what the country was coming to, but as soon as the alcohol got put in the sales started to go up again. People wanted to feel that burning sensation because when you're burning that means you're suffering, and everyone knows you've got to suffer in order to get better.

The poor copywriter? He's sitting there turning out the greatest campaign of all times that says this stuff doesn't burn – when burning happens to be the one thing you need to sell the product. It really isn't such an easy business at times.

The Hertz-Avis campaign is a classic in so many ways. According to people I've talked to, the Avis 'We Try Harder' campaign by Doyle, Dane was never meant to beat Hertz. But that's the way it looked in the ads and the commercials. When the Avis campaign began, Hertz was number one and Avis and National were running neck and neck for number two. But look how clever it was: Avis attacks the guy who is number one and makes it a one-two situation and nobody even remembers that National is still around. I really don't think Avis took all that many customers away from Hertz; they grabbed them off from National, from Olins, from Budget-Rent-A-Car, from all the smaller car-rentals companies who are running four, five, even number six to Hertz.

Everybody's looking at the ads and saying, Wow, what strategy, they're attacking Hertz! But they really weren't. What happened is that the guy who used to rent from the number-four outfit decides to trade up: he'll now try the number-two company. It also was a great campaign for the businessman who does a lot of renting of cars. He sits there and says to himself that his boiler-plate factory is maybe number six to American Standard and he feels sympathy for these Avis guys, so instead of going to National, he'll try Avis.

Now the Carl Ally people, who took over the Hertz account, were faced with the Avis problem. They helped Avis, really, because suddenly they acknowledged the existence of someone else in the field. For the first time the guy who was on top admitted that there was a guy under him. But they had to do this. Their surveys showed that the Hertz employees actually felt lousy about the Avis campaign, so it was necessary to come up with a campaign that answered Avis. In doing this, they helped cement the one-two situation that Avis had begun. They'll be teaching the Avis campaign in advertising classes for years. It was brilliant, and it will be a classic.

Next to destination advertising, the easiest kind of campaign to produce is public-service advertising. Anybody – but anybody – can write great public-service stuff. Every year agencies win all kinds of awards for their public-service campaigns and there's a reason why: the subject matter lends itself to dramatic advertising. I don't want to sound cynical, but think about it for a minute: you're talking about starving people, diseased people, Korean kids without families; you're talking about bigotry, about people who can't rent apartments; you're talking about Vietnam and nuclear explosions. Who couldn't do a great ad on rats and roaches in New York City housing?

I tell the kids who come in to see me for a job to write me ten public-service ads. The kids want to know what the story is. Well, the story is that in this terrible world there is always somebody starving. The children in Europe may not be starving but they're starving in Biafra. There are always kids starving someplace in the world. One kid produced an ad that said, 'There's more protein in a can of beer than a kid in Biafra gets in a week.' Another kid came into my office with an ad that said, 'You've got the cure to heart disease in your wallet.' I used to teach advertising at the School of Visual Arts and one of my students there produced this headline on an anti-Vietnam ad: 'Will Your Son Be a Light-to-Minor Casualty or a Heavy-to-Major Casualty?' Y. & R. did the great 'Give a Damn' campaign for the Urban Coalition in New York City. Great stuff. And someone produced a classic commercial showing a Negro trying to rent an apartment. The renting agent showing the apartment tries to flush the toilet but it doesn't work. 'Ah, a ten-cent washer will fix that,' he says. The place is falling apart, and the agent keeps pressing the Negro: 'Come on, are you going to take it or not? I've got people waiting to rent this place if you don't.' Very powerful stuff and beautifully done.

Where advertising starts to get tough is when all of the products are almost alike. If you take a close look, the rates on a lot of cars you rent are pretty much the same. For Hertz and Avis, they're almost identical. The plane fare to London is the same whether you fly Pan Am, TWA, BOAC. If you want to go to London by way of Iceland, then the fare is cheaper, but otherwise it's the same. So the advertising has to come up with the difference. When you look for differences, sometimes you have to stretch a bit. George Lois's agency – Lois, Holland, Callaway – did a series of commercials for Braniff using two celebrities sitting in a Braniff plane saying, 'When you've got it, flaunt it.'

Shep Kurnit, the president of Delehanty, Kurnit & Geller, once made a remark about that campaign that is pretty accurate: 'I wouldn't want to fly on the same plane with Andy Warhol or Sonny Liston.' Most people in advertising don't like the current Braniff campaign but that could be their jealousy of George Lois. I've got a feeling that the jury is still out on the campaign. 'Flaunt' is a very tough word for people to grasp. Actually, if you've got it, you usually don't flaunt it. I think that Mary Wells did a much better job with Braniff when she painted the airplanes because there was something real, something you could see.

What do you do with gasoline? There's very little brand loyalty in gasoline, so the companies are breaking their necks with their contests. The gas companies are in trouble and they know it. They know the consumer couldn't really care less what kind of gas he puts in his car. You're running out of gas and you go into a gasoline station. So to point up the difference they come up with lucky bucks, lucky dollars, the Presidents game, the antique-car game, the professional football players game and every other game they can think of. Not only are the games a must, but the government is going to make the rules for them a lot tougher. People realize you can't win, that the chances are one in a million of winning.

Mobil has a pretty good campaign going now, the one that says, 'We want you to live.' Shell is telling me I have to have Platformate. Esso, I don't even know what they're telling me – maybe they're still trying to shove tigers in your tanks. Somebody else is saying, 'Visit a gasoline station this week,' like it's a great experience. Other people are saying, 'Our rest rooms are terrific, you'd be proud to have them in your own home.' That's crazy. Nine-tenths of the rest rooms in this country are pigsties, and nowadays gas stations are putting in locks so you have to pay to use them.

Mobil is smarter than this. They've got games but they're also asking you not to wrap your car up. They want you to live long enough to play their game, which is the best of both worlds. Most of the gasoline companies play it safe and stick with the heavy, starchy agencies. The heavy agencies have difficulty with unique products; and with something like gas they're really stuck. A bright young agency might run into trouble with gas but at least they would approach it in a different way. A small agency, Smith/Greenland, got a shot at Flying A gasoline, and they turned out a very good job. Their pitch was that we design the gasoline for the way you drive in city traffic instead of country traffic. And they show a guy stuck on the Long Island Expressway someplace, trying to get through traffic. In the history of gasoline commercials, nobody has ever been stuck in a jam. You're always seeing guys zipping down empty roads at ninety miles an hour. No one has ever hinted that you can get stuck in traffic. The campaign was good: they told motorists that most driving in the city is stop-and-go and that Flying A is the best gasoline for such conditions. It was the first time a small agency had a chance to do something with gasoline and I think they did a good job. (In January 1970 the account moved from Smith/Greenland to Delehanty. My guess is it's because the copywriter who conceived the campaign, Helen Nolan, had herself just moved from Smith/Greenland to Delehanty.)

Of course some campaigns go bad for strange reasons. There's a big New York agency about to lose a very big account in the Midwest. Nobody talks about it, but what happened is that the agency guy was having an affair with the wife of the president of the account. He got caught, and his agency got him the hell out of town by promoting him to the presidency of the New York office, which as far as I'm concerned is the ultimate promotion. Despite the agency moving this guy out of town, they're still going to lose the account. Getting caught in the saddle is almost always grounds for losing an account.

CHAPTER THREE

FEAR, SON OF FEAR, AND FEAR MEETS ABBOTT AND COSTELLO

'Copywriters and art directors have cold periods. If they're not professionals about it, they show it, and they're cold out loud – I mean, they're cold to the whole world. They just can't come up with anything. Instead of cooling it and relaxing, they act cold and they lose it all. That's the time when the killers move in. They smell it. They smell it better than anybody else does. They know when a guy's about to die . . .'

One Friday night a guy working late at the Marvin, Scott, and Friml agency decided to pack it in and go home about 11 or 11:30 at night. He walked out of his office, and luckily there was an elevator at the elevator bank. This guy – he was an account man – looked around and there was no one in sight so he climbs into the elevator, closes the door and manages to get it down to the ground floor. He opened the door and stumbled out of the elevator, he was that tired.

Monday morning, someone comes into his office and asks him if he had been working late Friday night. The account man says yes he was, in fact until about 11:30 p.m. 'Did you sign out at eleven-twenty-five p.m.?' The guy says it was about that time he signed out. 'Well,' says the fellow, 'I don't know how to tell you this. I'm very sorry, but you're fired.' The account man was shocked and he says, 'For what?' The other guy says, 'I know it sounds crazy and I really don't know how to explain it to you, but you stole Marvin L. Marvin's *personal* elevator Friday night. That elevator you took was waiting there for him; it was his own elevator that took Marvin L. Marvin up and carried him down.' Marvin L. Marvin is the chairman of the agency, and this story, by the way, comes to you from another account man at the same agency who never worked late, so he had no problems.

Even if it's more fiction than fact, it still figures that the account guy in this case will probably go through life terrified to get in an elevator. The story also shows the kinds of craziness that go on on Madison Avenue and how fear can grow. In 1967 and 1968, when a large agency was going through a very, very tough shakeout to save their skin, they must have fired about six hundred people. Many of those six hundred people were secretaries, clerks, and so forth, but there must have been several dozen biggies. They all were on one floor –

and that floor was called 'The Floor of the Forgotten Men' by people in other agencies around town. The floor was manned by only one girl, who sat out front answering phones to give that last shred of dignity to those guys so they wouldn't have to answer their own phones. These were the Forgotten Men. They all had offices and they all were working out the employment contracts they had with this large agency.

These were top-money guys, account supervisors and management people, making fifty, sixty, seventy thousand dollars a year – the very top of the advertising business. None of them ever admitted that he was one of the fired people, but you know, they never had a secretary or anything. It was weird; they really didn't know whether it was the 'Floor of the Forgotten Men' but they had a pretty good notion. They would run around for interviews and the telephone would ring and the messages might come in, and at the end of the day when they were back that one receptionist would walk into an office and say, 'You've had messages.' They were walking around, but they were zombies. What I can't get over is that they never talked to each other about being fired. They all would show up for work at 9:30 in the morning, because that was the thing to do, and then they'd have to go to another floor to find the coffee machine because there wasn't a coffee machine on the 'Floor of the Forgotten Men'. Nobody ever said, 'Hey, I got a lead on something over at Kenyon and Eckhart.' A guy I know today was on that floor and he recently ran into another guy who was also on that floor at the same time. They started talking about it and they realized for the first time that they had been fired.

At that same time, over at Interpublic, Marion Harper, the chairman, was about to become a Forgotten Man himself. He revolutionized the business. They used to call him 'Marvel'

Harper, because he was. He took the concept that an agency ought to be an all-service organization and he built a gigantic company on this idea. He had a separate company to handle public relations for his clients, and he even had a research company to dream up new products which maybe were four years away from manufacturing. And then one day he got his. What happened was that six guys held a meeting in a conference room and they invited Harper to sit in on his own execution. And the amazing thing is, all of these guys had been brought in by Harper. They sat around and then one of them said, 'Marion, it's time. We want to take a vote.' It was a shock because although things were going bad, Harper never had considered a vote. He always thought he was strong enough even if they put it to a vote. So they voted. Six zips: one abstention. Harper abstained. It was like a Mafia meeting where they hit their hand and they come down with their thumb. It was the business world's kiss of death.

You see, they still were underlings, but put together they made one big overling. Harper made them strong enough to kill him. The Harper case was very rare, so rare it made the front pages. And today, Harper is trying for a comeback – he's still trying to put something together. (On January 30, 1970, it was announced that Marion was forming a new agency, along with Ron Rosenfeld, a copywriter, and Len Sirowitz, an art director.)

How do they tell somebody at Ted Bates that he's fired? I've had guys coming in to see me who say, 'I'm going to get it. Do you have anything here for me? I know I'm going to go because there was a meeting today on the account and they didn't invite me. They held an important meeting without asking me.' You know, it could be an oversight, it could be some secretary left this guy's name off a memo, it could be anything, but the guy immediately assumes that this is death, this is the end. Little by little, guys who thought he was great on new business don't say hello any more. They meet in the hallway and it's very fast. 'Hi, how are you?' and 'How's it going?' These guys who suddenly feel they're marked for death have to scramble to get attention again. They hustle around in hopes that they'll find a new account and they'll come back. They look for a chance.

If there is a jungle part to the advertising business, this is it – when a guy is wounded and trying to survive. But the word goes out, and there are a lot of people around town who can smell a guy who's going to die. And they jump him. They literally jump him. No holds are barred. The minute the guy looks like he's dead, he immediately becomes the butt of a lot of jokes. 'He could never do it; I always knew he was a bum.'

One agency president I know has a master plan for his entire agency. The president knows exactly when each person is going to get it. This president understands that if an underling gets too powerful or controls too big a piece of the business, then he, the president, is in trouble. So he's got a chart in his hand with a date of departure marked beside everyone's name. I once talked to an account man working for this president and I told him, 'You're dead because in the master plan everybody goes, you included.' This guy laughed. The last time I saw him he said, 'You know, you were right. He *does* have a master plan. Everybody goes. One by one, everybody gets it.'

The master plan works this way: 'This guy can take me up from a fashion agency to package goods where the real money is, but he can't take me past package goods. And this other guy, who got me a piece of cosmetic business, is my best friend and he's saved me and he's helped me make an agency and I love him and he's great, but if I ever get to be a fifty-million-dollar agency and Henry Ford walks in the door with his account, this guy can't carry it.'

Usually the large agencies have a killer to do the firing. Most agencies have one killer; the bigger agencies might have two killers. At Ted Bates & Company the agency killer was a little guy I'll call Billy, who started with Ted Bates when the agency opened in the early 1940s. He lived right through up to his retirement a few years ago. He fired hundreds of people in his lifetime and literally was the cause of more unhappiness than any man I know. From the outside, it didn't look like he had a big job at the agency, but he was the killer. And this guy did a job on everybody. He really was powerful, and he got his power by being close to Bates, the real Ted Bates. Who, by the way, really exists. Most people don't know that. The real Ted Bates is supposed to be very quiet and very shy and doesn't like to see people. He's the Howard Hughes of advertising. Most people think that Ted Bates is a guy by the name of Ted who met another guy by the name of Bates and when they got together they said, 'We'll call it Ted Bates.'

Rosser Reeves was the flamboyant genius who was out front. The guy who caused all the trouble was Billy. When he retired, they threw an enormous banquet for him and gave him a golden stiletto as a going-away gift. I'm kidding about the stiletto, but they were frightened of him. The Bates killer reportedly walked away with a cool million when he retired. Plus the golden stiletto. (People don't realize that advertising is the greatest welfare state going in the world. If you stay in one place long enough, you've got to pick up an enormous amount of bread. They may give you 5 percent of your annual salary and put it away for you in the profit-sharing plan, and this on top of the enormous salary and expense account.)

The Bates killer could fire anybody – and he had balls, too. He decided that he knew as much about writing and art directing as any creative person and that he would fire guys in every area of the agency. Guys lived in fear of him for years. He was considered the ultimate killer.

When I worked at Fuller & Smith & Ross they had a killer who was a combination killer and faggot. He really was. He would kiss you to death. He's dead now, but I don't hear many people grieving for him. Now this killer was the agency bookkeeper, the guy who was in charge of the money coming in and going out.

At one point they kept insisting that I fill out my time sheets – so many hours worked for such and such a client, that kind of thing. I insisted that I wouldn't fool around with the time sheets. Finally, it came to a point where petty cash owed me one hundred and fifteen dollars and I really needed the money. So I went to the faggot-killer and said, 'Joey, you know I'd like to have the money you owe me.' The killer said, 'Well, you're behind on your time sheets.' I said, 'Forget it. I'll give you a time sheet tomorrow. But give me the money now.' Joey said, 'No. Absolutely not. You're not getting your money until I see every time sheet here.' So I said, 'O.K. I'll leave and I'll get my money.' He said, 'How do you intend to get your money if I won't give it to you?' I said, 'I'm going to hock my typewriter.'

So I picked up my typewriter, put it under my arm, and started to walk out of the office. The faggot-killer spots me and starts screaming, 'I'll have you arrested if you take that typewriter.' Well, the creative director hears all this screaming – and nobody can scream like a faggot-killer – and he comes running out of his office and there was a big meeting. They decided to give me my money, but it was a draw because two days later I had to turn in my time sheets.

I think most agency killers pick the job for themselves. Nobody walks up to them and says, 'You look like a nasty bastard, you can be the killer here.' He doesn't have to have the power, that's the interesting part about it. Killers do things that eventually get them the job. Like they'll show unnecessary zeal in screwing a company out of fifty cents on some bill. Occasionally, killers split up their territory. One killer, for instance, will handle the account area and maybe media, and the other killer will take on the creative side of the agency. Very efficient, the agency killers. Sometimes, when an agency starts going downhill, the killers are so busy they can hardly keep up with the work.

In a lot of ways they're very much like the guys in the Mafia. You know, hit guys are not bad guys at all. They're friendly toward dogs and little kids; in fact, they're real nice except for the fact that they kill. Killers for some strange reason usually aren't top management. They're either running a piece of the production department, or the media department, or, like the faggot-killer, in accounting and bookkeeping. They're medium-level guys.

Killers don't make the actual decision to kill, but they'll egg somebody on to make the decision. They're the people who say, 'You know, Harry over there hasn't turned out a decent ad in the last six months. I don't know what we're doing with a guy like that.' Harry, who's uptight for his own crazy reasons, suddenly hears the word that he hasn't turned out an ad for six months, which makes him so nervous that he then doesn't turn out an ad for still another six months. At the end of the year, Harry's out.

Copywriters and art directors have cold periods. If they're not professionals about it, they show it, and they're cold out loud – I mean, they're cold to the whole world. They just can't come up with anything. Instead of cooling it and relaxing, they act cold and they lose it all. That's the time when the killers move in. They smell it. They smell it better than anybody else does. They know when a guy's about to die. Killers flourish best at agencies really on their way down and also at agencies growing like hell and getting bigger by the moment. So one killer is killing out of fear and the other type is killing out of, maybe, impatience. They want their agency to grow faster than Mary Wells has. And if every new guy who shows up doesn't start producing immediately, the killer wants them taken care of. Killers are almost an integral part of an agency today.

It's a little bit like the old West. A guy's reputation is the first thing you hear about. Let's say you're brought to a new agency, and usually somebody walks up to you that first week and he says, 'Hi, my name is So-and-so and I work here.' Invariably, inevitably, the conversation gets around to 'Watch out for that guy.' Then your new friend says, 'This is a nice place and I like it. You can't get much work out, but don't worry about it.' Then, all of a sudden it's like a prison movie: 'That guy over there, that little bastard, watch out for him.' This is the language of the business. Then you know that the guy he's talking about is the killer. You know that he's the guy who will do the job on you if the job ever has to be done.

Let's say a creative director has got himself a bad art director who has to go. Since the creative director hired the art director, the chances are that *he's* afraid, so he's not going to go blabbing around that 'I blew it with Joe over there, I made a bad decision and shouldn't have hired him.' The creative director is beyond all that. The agency president? He's so far removed from everything that he's really out of advertising. He's spending most of his time with a couple of guys who run a boiler room who claim they're going to take his agency public and make everybody a bundle. The account supervisor is so scared of losing the account that he can barely talk, much less think straight. So the actual job falls to someone between the account supervisor and the creative supervisor. The way it's done is that the creative supervisor will mumble something to the killer which goes like this: 'You know, Joe isn't behaving too well lately.' Then the account supervisor screws up his courage and he might stammer to the killer, 'Yeah, Joe is acting up, he came in at ten yesterday morning and he was drunk. He's got to go.' The killer mops up.

Some killers eventually kill off so many people that the board of directors decides on a change of management. Then a whole new crew of guys is brought in, and the new guys don't realize that they have a killer on their hands. That's when the killers get it. Whenever a killer gets hit in an agency, or when he retires, there's a celebration – a real party.

The retirement party for the Bates killer was marvelous. Practically the whole agency showed up for it. First of all, everyone had a great deal of respect for the guy – you know, here we have a tried and true survivor. And secondly, nobody's going to screw around and not show up because who knows, maybe he'll get bored by retirement and he'll come back to work at the agency. Nobody wanted to risk a scene like that. Even in retirement the guy struck fear into people.

When I worked at Daniel & Charles there were so many going-away parties for guys who got fired that I figured out a way to ease the financial burden on those people who had to kick in five or ten dollars every week for the party. I decided to sell insurance. I went around to the creative department and said, 'Give me three dollars out of your paychecks every week and I'll book it. The next time somebody gets it I'll pay for the party.'

There was a copywriter there named Marvin who was doing quite nicely with his accounts. One day he got into a conversation with some other people in the creative department who said, 'Marvin, you're being underpaid. You're doing a hell of a job and they're killing you when it comes to bread. Frankly, Marvin, you're worth a lot more.'

Now they weren't egging this guy on, they honestly thought that the guy was doing a job and deserved a better deal. Marvin says, 'Holy shit, you're right, I'm going to go in there and talk to Charlie.' Charlie Goldschmidt was one of the two owners of the agency and is the chairman of the board. Well, he went in to talk to Charlie and Charlie says. 'Marvin, that's very funny, I wanted to talk to you.' And then Charlie fired Marvin. Marvin was going to be fired all along; if he had kept quiet he would have lasted a few more weeks.

Charlie was doing a lot of firing those days. On one day there were account assignments coming out and Charlie had to pencil in assignments for everyone. He pencils in a lot of names and then when he comes to a guy named Dennis, he doesn't pencil Dennis's name in but rather he puts down 'Mr. X' to work on such and such an account. In his mind, of course, he was about to fire Dennis. The only problem is that on the list are Dennis's accounts and next to Dennis's name is 'Mr. X.' Of course he hadn't gotten around to tell Dennis that he was out and 'Mr. X' was coming in. And of course his secretary, she doesn't know anything, so she goes ahead, types the list out, and the account list is circulated throughout the agency. The next scene: Charlie running all over the agency trying to grab back these things from everybody including Dennis. Well, he wasn't fast enough – the legs go first on an agency president – and when Charlie gets to Dennis's office, there's Dennis, white, looking at the list. 'I'm sorry,' said Charlie, 'I'm sorry you had to find out this way.' Charlie had not been able to find a replacement for Dennis and didn't want to fire him until he did.

Charlie liked me and when I told him I was leaving he was quiet for two weeks. On the next to the last day he came into my office and said, 'Kid, can't you change your mind? Kid, what can I do for you? Kid, you could own this place someday.' Last day, he's in my office again. I shook his hand and said, 'Goodbye, Charlie.' 'Goodbye, kid,' he says. 'I wish you luck, but you're making a mistake.'

I went downstairs for a going-away drink with everybody. A guy comes running down saying, 'You got to go upstairs again. Charlie's gone berserk; he's firing everybody. So help me. Go upstairs.'

And he was. Charlie had simply gone into the office of a fellow named Mike Lawlor and said, 'Mike, are you going to follow Jerry?' Mike says, 'No, Charlie, I wouldn't do anything like that.' Charlie says, 'Mike, are you going to take your book [meaning portfolio] up to Fuller & Smith & Ross?' 'I might,' says Mike. Lawlor felt that the Bill of Rights allowed a guy to show his book around town. 'Get out of here,' says Charlie. 'You're fired. Pack up your things and get out.' He then went into the office of a guy named Bert Klein and said, 'Bert, you're Jerry's friend, aren't you?' 'Yeah.' 'Are you going to follow him?' 'Gee, I don't know.' 'Did you ever have your book up to that agency?' 'Yeah, I've had my book up there.' 'Get out,' said Charlie, 'you're fired.' Still another friend of mine, a guy named Bob Tore, was coming out of the men's room. He was a little wobbly because he had heard that Charlie was going from office to office firing people. Charlie grabbed this guy Bob and said, 'You're Jerry's friend, aren't you?' Poor Bob. He starts to stammer, 'Uh, uh, yeah,

I know Jerry . . .' Charlie got compassionate: 'Never mind. You got two kids. I won't fire you.'

Charlie, who now is a good friend of mine, really did a job that day. I don't know what the final head count was, but he put in a good day's work. The next day he had four free-lancers working up there to take up the slack. And the guys he fired were no slouches. Mike Lawlor went to Doyle, Dane, Bert Klein to Wells, Rich.

One of the reasons for all the chaos is that, suddenly, an account can pull out of an agency. An account has to give an agency ninety days' notice before it pulls out. I swear there are some guys on Madison Avenue who hide in the bathroom on Friday. Friday is kill day because it's the end of the week – killing is done on Friday for bookkeeping reasons. What's so sad about it is that the wrong guys get fired. Management calls in some poor guy and says, in effect, 'As you know, we've just blown fifteen million dollars worth of billing, and your one hundred and sixty bucks a week stands between us and survival.' It's almost ludicrous. Agencies net 15 percent of the account's billing, plus a little extra from things like production charges. Agency blows $15 million in billing, which adds up to like $2,500,000 to the agency and they go to the guy who's making eight or nine grand a year and they tell him, 'Look, things are very bad and we're going to have to let you go.' The guy who's saying this, by the way, is making forty or fifty big ones a year and he's usually safer. There seems to be a rule of thumb, written somewhere, that the guy making thirty thousand or better is much safer than the guy making eleven.

It's a terrible system and one of the results of it is the guy who makes that thirty or forty grand a year is a very nervous cat. Although he really is safer, he has so much more to lose.

He cries a lot at night. During the day you can spot him breezing out of the agency for a fifty-minute pick-me-up from his shrink. God knows how many people on Madison Avenue go to the shrinks, but the number and percentages must be enormous. You see everyone zipping out on Wednesday afternoon, two to three, for a fix. They come back and they're acting like real people again. They're O.K.

If you get into a discussion with somebody about his shrink, he clams up. Going to the shrink is not any status thing. People get very uptight about their shrinks. Oh, someone might casually remember that once, about ten years ago, he paid a short visit to a shrink, but that's about it. The advertising guy goes to the shrink because he's worried about losing his account. The shrink is probably sneaking off to *his* shrink because *he's* worried about losing all of those advertising guys who shell out the bucks. So the shrink has to hold the advertising guy; the advertising guy has to hold the account. Everybody's holding on for dear life. The day is going to come when a bunch of shrinks decide that they ought to start an agency.

It's not tough to figure out why there is so much fear in advertising. It's my theory that much of the fear starts very, very casually. Let's say the wife of the chairman of a board of a large company is sitting under the hair dryer one day and she hears a couple of chicks talking about a funny Volkswagen commercial. At dinner that night she starts nagging her husband. He's got enough headaches as it is, what with trying to get a new line of credit that won't be usury, and also thinking he's developing a heart condition. Anyhow, there's his wife whining, 'Harry, oh Harry, why can't your company have funny little commercials like they do for Volkswagen?' He feels a little pain in his chest and he mumbles something at her.

Next day, he's out of sorts and the president of his company walks in, and the chairman says to the president, 'Listen, Fritz, why don't we get some advertising here? I sign a lot of bills. We spend three million dollars a year on advertising. What have we got to show for it?' The president suddenly feels that creepy little chill and says, 'My God, Harry, you're right!'

The president suddenly trots down to the advertising manager and says, 'You know, Don, I wonder if it isn't about time that we reevaluate our advertising. We've been with Winthrop, Saltonstall, Epstein and Gambrelli now for four years. They still haven't turned out a campaign that we can be proud of and happy with.' Now who's going to stop passing the buck? The advertising manager, who's making maybe eighteen or twenty grand a year and up to his ears in a mortgage in Tenafly, isn't about to say to the president of the company. 'You're wrong.' Nor is the president about to say to the chairman, 'Now, Harry, I think maybe you're wrong about our advertising, why don't you take a Cert or a Tum or something and settle down?'

So that fatal telephone call is made. The advertising manager calls two or three agencies he's been keeping his eye on and says, very casually, 'Wonder if you fellows would like to come over and talk to us? We've been reevaluating our advertising and . . . Now we're very happy with Winthrop etc., don't get me wrong about that, we just thought we'd take a look at some other approaches . . .'

Whammo! As soon as two or three agencies get the word, that word leaks out. I don't know why, but pretty soon everybody in town knows it. There hasn't been a new account change in years that was a surprise. The word finally reaches one of the advertising publications. Is it true that Ford is looking for a new agency? Well now, you're at Thompson working on the Ford account and your life goes before your eyes. You see that in two or three months you're going to be out of work, and in advertising when you're on the beach it usually lasts for eight or nine months.

For the sake of argument, let's say the word doesn't get out. Maybe you just sense that the chairman of the board might have talked to the president. Maybe, just maybe, there's a meeting and you get a feeling: 'I don't like the way Don smiled at me when he left that meeting.' I've seen guys standing around after a meeting saying, 'Did you notice that his last words were, "I'll see you. It's been nice knowing you"? What did he mean by that?' Then somebody else pipes up and says, 'Obviously, he's trying to scare us.' Another guy says, 'Fuck him, he can't scare us.' And you know what? It hits them. The next day everybody's sitting around wondering how they're going to lose that account. Still another guy says, 'Remember looking at that guy from the account? He didn't smile during the presentation.' Then they start at each other: 'Why did you talk so much?' 'I didn't talk so much; *you* spent too much time talking to the guy who didn't smile.' 'I didn't talk that much; you screwed up the slide projector. No wonder that guy didn't smile.'

Now let's take the other side of what can happen. Let's say that the advertising manager decides to tell his agency that things aren't going well. The opposite of when the word doesn't get out officially; that is, the account executive is told – point-blank – that he's in trouble, and he doesn't have to go through all the mumbo jumbo of figuring out who didn't smile at a meeting.

So Don, the advertising manager, meets with the account executive and says, 'Joe, I had a little session with the president yesterday and look, I don't want you people to get nervous but he's really not too pleased with the way things are going.' The blood starts to drain out of Joe's face and his fingers go numb. He starts to nod and stutters, 'Well, Don, don't worry, we'll work something out.' Joe runs back to the agency like Paul Revere screaming 'The British are coming. The British are coming.' He's screaming, 'We're in trouble, we're in trouble.' Guys begin running around. There are dozens of meetings. The whole thing is weird to watch because when that account man comes back and they close that door and he says, 'Look, we're in a lot of trouble, the president of the company says our ads are lousy,' that's the first sign of death.

Whichever way the word comes – directly from the advertising manager or indirectly from gossip in the trade papers or from something you pick up at a meeting – it immediately spreads throughout the entire agency. I was a mailboy at Ruthrauff & Ryan when they were on their way to losing the Kentile account. The kids working in the mailroom making sixty bucks a week knew a year ahead that Ruthrauff & Ryan was going to lose the account and they were scared stiff. And you know, the kids were right, Kentile moved out of there in like ten months. Ruthrauff & Ryan is gone today – nothing, it doesn't exist. One of the reasons that it died was because of no communication. The mailroom knew they were going to lose accounts before the management did.

They were an old-fashioned agency, old-line, and they just dribbled away to nothing. When I went to work there in 1955 the big news was they hired a guy who 'had a great book of names.' I didn't know what the hell that meant and then it dawned on me: they went and hired a guy who was more of a pimp than he was an account executive. This was the guy with a big fat address book who was going to save them. I mean, forget it, this guy knew how to get anybody in town fixed up. Blue movies. He's got it. Blondes, brunettes or redheads, he has them. You know, I really was impressed as hell. This guy was to be the agency whoremaster. And the talk about this guy: 'He's going to bring us the business.' They honestly thought a cat like that was going to save them. And there are agencies around today with a somewhat similar attitude. Glad-hand the account. Get the account tickets to the Giants' football games. Big dinners at '21' and Le Pavillon. The weak agencies, fearful of losing an account, will resort to anything to keep the account. The hot agencies, they don't need this. What does Doyle, Dane need with a whoremaster? They're turning out terrific work. What does Delehanty, Kurnit need with a guy like this? Or Wells; Rich, Greene? These people are professionals doing a good job.

Now sometimes an account takes advantage of all this fear of losing an account. TWA is the classic example. In 1967 TWA was at Foote, Cone & Belding, and they were doing a pretty good job on the account. Most of the airlines are losing money hand over foot, not because their advertising is good or bad, but because the Government has screwed up the business so. The airlines live on Government handouts and subsidies and on airmail contracts. And the Government tells the airlines where to fly. Give me an airline that the Government says *must* fly to Buffalo and I'll show you an airline losing money. I mean, nobody goes to Buffalo. Anyhow, someone gets itchy at TWA and they decide that maybe what they need, besides a couple of routes to Hawaii, is some new advertising. So they call up Foote, Cone and say, 'You're a swell bunch of guys, Foote, Cone, but we're not that happy ...'

I guess TWA at that time was billing $22 million. Do you understand what that means to an agency? Any agency?

Something like $4 million a year in income. Well, the panic spread through Foote, Cone like wildfire. I was a creative supervisor at Ted Bates at the time and the calls started coming in. Copywriters, art directors, creative people – the big scare was on. That afternoon I met a girl from Foote, Cone in a restaurant and she said, 'It's true, it's happening. We're going to lose it – in a day or so.' She was petrified. She was making forty grand a year as a writer and TWA was the only account she was working on, and she had to find a job fast. She had a whole list of people she was going to see about a job.

What happened in those next few weeks was the second most public rape since the Sabine women got it. Never before in the history of advertising were so many guys taken at the same time. TWA really did a first-rate job. A lot of very smart, very wise guys got taken. The whole thing was a big flimflam.

TWA was looking for freebies – presentation of agencies' work without paying the freight. To get the freebies they went to nervous agencies – Dancer-Fitzgerald-Sample; Benton & Bowles; Ted Bates. And they were such nice guys they even let the poor bastards at Foote, Cone compete for their own account. William Esty, N.W. Ayer, Sullivan Stauffer, and even McCann-Erickson were in there, too. They went to the old-line agencies who were beginning to feel the pinch from the new agencies coming up. Now these old-line agency fellows are not dummies; they're sharpies.

I don't know how many guys called TWA and said, 'We want in on the presentation,' and I don't know which ones were called specifically by TWA and told, 'We'd like you in on this.' TWA was pretty smooth, too. They never would come out and say go out and spend $40,000 or $50,000 on a commercial. No, they would say, 'We'd like to see some examples of your work, the work you would be doing for us.'

TWA never said, 'Don't spend the bread.' They just smiled and sucked everyone in.

They didn't get any response from outfits like Doyle, Dane. Or Ogilvy. Or Mary Wells. Agencies like these show possible new business what they've really done in the past and let it go at that. If anyone ever asked Doyle, Dane for a sample campaign, Doyle, Dane would say, 'We don't play that way.' They turn out great work; they win awards every year from their fellow workers. They're good and they know it.

All of a sudden this thing snowballed, snowballed right out of sight. Everyone started out by saying, 'Well, we'll give them a few sketches, maybe a handful of roughs.' Then another guy would say, 'Well, look, you know we're up against those guys at Bates. You know what sharpies they are. Let's go for a little more than a sketch. Let's go look for a shot.' And the next guy says, 'Well, look, if we're taking shots for a print ad, we just can't walk over there with a storyboard. You know how tough it is to show storyboards.' And another guy says, 'I know a guy who would shoot this commercial for twenty thousand dollars.' Guys suddenly went into business working on the TWA account without having it.

Long about then a skinny kid named Jim Webb with a lot of hair was out on the West Coast starting out as a songwriter. If this kid knew what chaos he caused in New York, he'd break up. One of the songs he wrote was called 'Up, Up, and Away' and it's got lines in it like 'Wouldn't you like to fly/in my beautiful balloon?' and stuff like that. Well, a chase develops for the commercial rights to this song. A group called the Fifth Dimension had recorded it, and it was very big about then. The infighting over that song! Also, the word leaked out that TWA hated their current song and this one seemed ideal. Anyhow, Foote, Cone somehow latched onto it, but as soon as the others heard that Foote, Cone had a song, then everyone else had to have a song.

You can't believe the Mickey Mouse stuff that went on at Bates during all this. I don't know what was doing at the other agencies, but at Bates it was crazy all the way. Doors were locked. Delivery boys used to show up with food orders from the delicatessen and couldn't get in – all Mickey Mouse. I remember one of the biggies running down the hall with a record cover – this guy was making maybe one hundred grand a year – and he's saying, 'This is the song, this is the one that's going to get us the account.' There was false elation that was almost sick. There was this absolutely positive feeling that *we* had it locked.

Well, everyone presents. Who knows how much money was spent on everybody's presentations? Upward of a million dollars would be my rough guess. Anyhow, everyone presents, and here's Foote, Cone with this beautiful song, which they've changed now to 'Up, Up, and Away – TWA,' and here's everyone else with real commercials, real print ads, the works. This kid Webb wrote a hell of a song and after looking at all of these presentations, TWA lets all the Sabine women have it. 'Nice work,' they say, and then they say, 'Foote, Cone, you've done such a hell of a job that we're going to keep the account with you.'

At Bates, when they learned what happened, it was like V-J Day, except that they were like the Japs, falling on swords. Unbelievable.

About six months later there was some kind of shake-up at TWA. A new guy with a lot of clout moved in and *he* decided that despite 'Up, Up, and Away – TWA' the account really didn't belong at Foote, Cone. So beautiful Mary Wells, who had just finished painting all the Braniff Airline planes fuchsia and colors like that, walks in – and off with the account. No formal presentation, nothing. Maybe she showed them a fuchsia plane, but nothing more. And she got it. To get the account and avoid a conflict of interest, she had to resign the Braniff account. And the president of Braniff is her husband.

George Lois, who used to be at Papert, Koenig and Lois and then started Lois, Holland, Callaway, is minding his own business and pretty soon there comes Braniff, fuchsia planes and all. It's not that all of advertising business is crazy, but there are times, there are times . . . And it is the craziness that leads to the nervousness that leads to the real fear on Madison Avenue. The TWA story must have driven twenty guys to drink, and it isn't all that unique a situation. There will always be nervousness wherever big money is at stake. And above everything else, Madison Avenue is big money.

CHAPTER FOUR

GIVE ME YOUR DRUNKS, YOUR WEIRDOS . . .

'Advertising is the only business in the world that takes on the lamed, the drunks, the potheads, and the weirdos. You can't make it as an account executive with a reputation for being a pothead, but you can probably last in the copy business or as an art director if your pupils are a little dilated. Eccentrics are drawn to the business and welcomed into it. Your best grade of eccentric is normally found on the creative side, among the copywriters and art directors . . .'

We get a great number of nutsy guys. Let's say that there are hundreds – maybe thousands – of guys in this business who, if they were working for Bankers Trust right now, would have found themselves committed. You know, their boss would have sat back and decided, 'This guy is really going,' and he would call the guy's wife up and say, 'I think it's time we committed him because, you know, he's doing strange things.'

Take a good friend of mine, Ned Viseltear, for example. He's really a legend. And yet he managed to get good job after good job.

Ned once worked for Grey Advertising for three hours. He had been hired as a copywriter and he goes into work at nine in the morning. Because Grey is a very straight-arrow kind of place, Ned shows up at work on the first day right on time – nine o'clock. He meets some people, fills out all the forms you have to fill out on the first day on a job and then around 12:15 he goes out to lunch. He had a date with someone at Daniel & Charles. Well, they had a nice lunch and the guy from Daniel & Charles says, 'Why don't you come to work at Daniel & Charles as a copywriter?' They get down to specifics and Ned is offered a job – better than the one he's got at Grey. So he goes down to Daniel & Charles, meets Danny Karsch, the other owner of that agency and the chairman of the executive committee, accepts the offer at about two in the afternoon.

But he couldn't resist picking up the phone. He's still up at Daniel & Charles and he dials Grey and asks for personnel. He says, 'My name is Ned Viseltear. I was working for you this morning. I worked for you for approximately three and a half hours.' And the woman on the other side says, 'Yes, what can I do for you?' Viseltear says, 'I'm quitting Grey. I'm leaving and taking another job.' The lady is getting a little uneasy with this guy on the phone, she thinks maybe he's some kind of a nut and pretty soon he'll start breathing heavily. Viseltear says, 'Well, I just wanted to know, have I accumulated any vacation time? I know I've only been working at Grey for three and a half hours, but if there's any vacation money due me I wish you'd send it to me in care of Daniel and Charles.'

In 1961 Daniel & Charles was like a school, except all the kids in the school seemed to be crazy. It was my first real job in advertising, I mean my first legitimate job. I had been out of work for seven months before going there and before I was out of work I had been writing hernia ads for a small outfit called the Advertising Exchange. I was living in Brooklyn and had no bread whatsoever. My relatives used to have my wife and me over to dinner. Sitting around the table, some uncle would say, 'Hey, kid, I see by the *Chief* [the Civil Service newspaper in New York City] that they got some openings coming up in the Sanitation Department. Why don't you forget this advertising bug and get yourself a job?'

I really didn't have the heart – or the stomach – for the Sanitation Department. So I sat around in my apartment in Brooklyn and tried to get something going. I decided that Daniel & Charles was the agency for me. I had been going through a book called the *Advertising Agency Register*, which lists all of the agencies in the business, and I was down to the *D*'s. I started sending them in roughs of sample ads. I just sent them in to Danny Karsch, one of the agency's partners, but without a name, just my initials, J.D.F. Anyhow, I kept sending those ads in and one day I called Daniel & Charles and asked for Danny. When the secretary asked who it was, I said, 'I'm J.D.F.' Danny had me come up for an interview and he hired me at one hundred dollars a week.

I found that the whole place was filled with young guys

who suddenly discovered that somebody was going to pay them a lot of money for the rest of their lives for doing this thing called advertising, and all of us got caught up in the insanity of it and went crazy. A whole group of people slowly went out of their skulls.

The first day I was at work we were sitting around in an art director's office and a guy came running into the office, screaming, 'Channel Eight, Channel Eight, there's something on Channel Eight.'

With this the room, which was full of guys, emptied. They literally ran over me. They ran down the hall and I followed them and when they got to the end of the hall they opened the doorway that led to the stairwell. Daniel & Charles was located on Thirty-fourth Street, about ten feet away from an apartment building. It was almost as if they were connecting buildings. From the stairwell these guys were able to look right into the apartment building, and they had designated the various apartments as Channel One, Channel Two, and so forth. Channel Eight was a very *zaftig*-looking young girl who happened to be walking around in her bra at the time – and nothing else. And like everybody was standing there, you know, commenting on the chick, throwing lines like, 'I don't think she's as nice as Channel Five.' This was my initiation into advertising.

There were guys at Daniel & Charles who were so addicted to those windows that they spent hours keeping an eye on the channels. The funniest sight and the funniest sound in the world was when we would be working late at night – after 10:00 p.m. – and you would hear a copywriter, Evan Stark, pushing his typewriter table down the hall to the stairwell and setting up the typewriter so he could write and watch at the same time. Bob Tore, the art director Evan worked with, would sit on the steps and the two of them would stare out the window and work on ads, but keeping an eye peeled to see what they could find. Evan would sit there and think of something and he would type because he would never work with a pencil. He would sit there and type a headline, always checking the windows, and finally one day Charlie Goldschmidt caught everybody.

There was a great confrontation, and because Charlie used to blame me for most of the crazy stuff in the agency he called me down and said, 'Well, Jerry, you and your gang have finally done it. The neighbors have called the cops and they say I've got an organization of Peeping Toms working here.' And I said, 'Charlie, I don't know what you're talking about.' And really, I didn't understand. He says, 'Well, you and your guys finally did it.' 'Charlie,' I said, 'you're out of your skull.' He said, 'You better go up and tell your gang they're in a lot of trouble.'

I ran upstairs and the first guy I saw was an art director named Bill Arzonetti, and I said, 'Bill, we're in trouble. Charlie says that there's an organized gang of Peeping Toms at Daniel and Charles.' Bill looked at me with a straight face and said, 'Gee, that's the first time I ever belonged to anything organized.'

Bill is an unusual guy. Very quiet, very good art director. One day I was working with him, and actually it was the first time we really had done any ads together. Anyhow, we're working away and his phone started to ring. Bill is a very uptight guy when he's working and he keeps working and ignores the phone. Couple of minutes pass. The phone is still ringing. I look at the phone but since I'm new I figure maybe Bill likes a phone to ring for five minutes before he picks it up. It's still ringing and he still doesn't answer it but I can see he's getting tenser and tenser, and he's just building up to an explosion. Finally he looks around and picks up a pair of scissors and he stabs the phone. Not simply cut the wire or anything like that. I mean he stabbed it, right from the handpiece all the way through the rest of it. 'That should hold it,' he said.

I looked at him and then I said, 'I think I hear somebody calling me. I'll be right back.' I didn't come back for two days. We still meet now and then and laugh about it. How many guys stab their telephones? He didn't kid around with it, either, I mean he wanted to *kill* that phone. The funny thing is that even after he stabbed it, it still rang. Bill was much calmer after he stabbed it.

We had another art director at Daniel & Charles – I'll call him Jack. One day Jack decided to leave his wife. He went home and told her, 'I'm leaving you. I have a girl friend.' His wife says, 'How can you do this to me?' Jack says, 'I have a girl friend.' His wife collapsed into a chair and started beating her breast, shouting, 'Why, why?' And he said, 'Well, what's wrong with having a girl friend? Look, all the other guys at the agency have girl friends. Why can't I have one?'

She decided to go gunning for everyone at the agency. Somehow she got a list of the agency people with their home phone numbers and she decided that she would call all of the wives and tell them that all of their husbands were running around. Then Jack told us that she decided not to make the phone calls, but instead she was going out to buy a gun and shoot everyone at the agency. We all started to look around for a good place to hide when she showed up. In the back of the creative department there was a closet with a false wall, and Bob Tore and I decided that if we ever heard gunfire or anything going on we would jump into this closet and stay there until it blew over. You may think I'm kidding but she was quoted as saying, 'I'm going to go up and get everybody.'

You can't really compare Jack with a guy like George Lois, who uses his wildness to get a lot of things done. There are literally hundreds of George Lois stories around town. George is a big husky Greek guy who has a hell of a temper, plus the fact that he's very, very creative and a hell of a good art director. All of these factors rolled into one tend to make things very exciting when George is around.

There are a couple of classic stories on Madison Avenue involving art directors trying to stuff their immediate superiors out a window. The way I heard one of these stories, an art director once tried to throw Norman B. Norman out of a window in the *Look* building, but the casement windows stopped him, along with an assist from another art director, named Onofrio Paccione.

There is a great, great nut in town I'll call Riley. He was a very good copywriter for Doyle, Dane. One day he went out to lunch and got very, very drunk and started feeling sorry for himself. He finally said the hell with the whole business, and when he came back from lunch he started to bust up his office. You know, throwing lamps around, breaking the chair. His method of getting the whole thing over with was not to leave Doyle, Dane but to destroy everything that was in there. The desk was the last piece that he wanted to do the job on.

He lifted up the window and started to shove his desk out of it. Well, those desks can weigh anywhere from a hundred pounds on up. Anyhow, all the racket that Riley was making busting up the chairs attracted attention. People started running into his office and the first thing they see is Riley, about to get a hernia, with his desk halfway out the window and about to go all the way out. A couple of guys tackle him and another couple of guys tackle the desk and manage to save a few lives. For years people would talk about Riley and his desk, and one day I asked him if the story were true. 'Hey, Riley, did you really try to do it? Did you really try to throw your desk out the window?' And he said, 'Yeah, but it was only on the Forty-third Street side of the building.' I mean, how can you help loving a guy who realizes that if his desk goes out on the Forty-second Street side it causes a lot of headaches, but it's O.K. on the Forty-third Street side. That's a very rational man.

I wouldn't want to give the impression that all the creative guys in town are crazy. I actually know of only one stabbing that ever took place, I mean besides the stabbing of the telephone. An art director named Angie once got into an argument with an account man over an ad and they started yelling at each other so Angie simply stabbed the account guy with a ballpoint pen. Oh, I guess there was a lot of blood and screaming, but the account guy lived. The agency decided they had to do something to Angie, so he was officially censured at a Plans Board meeting, which is composed of the most influential people in an agency. The account guy recovered nicely and then took out a Major Medical policy. I see Angie every now and then. I ran into him just the other day on Fifty-ninth Street, looking very strange. He was carrying his coat under one arm, his shirt was not tucked in his pants, he had a three-day growth of beard, and I don't think he had been home for a while.

On the whole, there's not that much violence. Once, on the New York Central, an agency president got into an argument about politics with the guy sitting next to him, and the next thing you knew, the president hit the guy a good shot in the mouth.

George Lois was involved in a small brawl with a friend of mine, Bill Casey. Casey had been working at Papert, Koenig, Lois and he was leaving. There was some kind of stock dispute about his leaving and so they scheduled a reconciliation meeting. Casey was the kind of guy who might have a couple of drinks in a bar and all of a sudden a brawl seems to erupt around him. Something went wrong at the reconciliation meeting and the first thing you know Lois vaults over a table and tries to take a punch at Casey. Secretaries were yelling, the usual chaos. It wasn't the greatest example of a guy leaving an agency. Casey then sued Lois, Julian Koenig, the whole bunch of them, on the grounds that 'an atmosphere of physical violence' kept him from doing his work at the agency.

He might have had something, because back in 1965 there was a terrific fight at PKL during which an account supervisor named Bert Sugar slugged another guy, leaving blood all over the place. They used to call PKL 'Stillman's East,' after the old fight gym.

If I were told to make a choice, I would say that copywriters are the craziest of all of the creative people. I once had a kid named Herb working for me when I was at Delehanty, a great nut. He was on everything in the world, you name it – speed, acid, grass, God knows what else. He used to come into the office looking very strange. It got to the point where if I had to stare into his dilated pupils one more time I would go crazy. I mean, he was bad news. But he was a hell of a good writer, so I kept him on.

The real problem with Herb was not the condition that he arrived in, but when he arrived. He used to come into the office at four o'clock in the afternoon. He used to tell me that he was afraid of the morning, that he hated the morning, so he would stay in bed until three or four and then go to work. It wasn't that he was shirking or anything – he used to work until midnight or one in the morning – it was just that he was working a different schedule.

Well, the problems started. Art directors were constantly looking for him and of course he was in bed. Account guys were always trying to pin him down, and there he was, breezing in at four in the afternoon, more likely than not zonked out, and account guys never did know how to handle zonked guys. And then the other copywriters saw Herb and the hours he was working and they wanted to work at night, too, and sleep in the morning.

I used to tell him, 'Herb, you've got to come in a little earlier. People are looking for you after ten in the morning, you know that, don't you?' Herb said, 'I can't help it. I'll do anything else you want, but I can't help it – I just have to come in at four or five in the afternoon.' I said, 'Herb, listen, you're going to be fired if you keep it up.' And he wouldn't listen.

We finally had to get rid of the guy because he was causing too much trouble. The day I decided to fire him he comes into my office. 'Jerry,' he says, 'I figured out how to get in early. I want a raise.'

This surprised me a little so I asked him what he meant.

'I've got a girl friend and I need the raise so that she can leave her apartment and move in with me. If she moves in with me she'll wake me up in the morning because she isn't afraid of the morning like I am and then I'll be able to get in to work on time. I won't oversleep.'

I said, 'Herb, you need more money from me so that your girl friend can move in and then she can wake you up, right?'

'Yes,' he said.

I said, 'Herb, did you ever hear of an alarm clock?'

'Did you ever try to fuck an alarm clock?' he said.

Herb went from Delehanty to several agencies where he did good work and always got fired, and he's someplace else now where he's about to get fired. He's been fired from some of the best agencies in town. One guy, at still another agency, fired him in the traditional Mafia method. He went out and bought a big fish and came back to the office and put it on Herb's desk. That was this guy's way of telling Herb he was through.

Many, many copywriters are paranoids. Herb felt that people and things were always rejecting him. One day he put a piece of paper into the Xerox machine at Delehanty to make a copy. Everybody was coming up to the Xerox machine and putting their pieces of paper in it and getting copies, but when Herb tried it there were some strange sounds and the original came out of the machine all ripped up. He picked it up, looked up, and said, 'Even the Xerox machine rejects me.'

There are hundreds of these guys floating through New York. One of them, named Wilder, has worked for practically every agency in the city. You hire Wilder and the next day he comes running down the hall barefooted, screaming, and causing a lot of commotion. He shows up at strange hours, doing very strange things. He keeps getting jobs because he's fairly good.

There's another guy named Harry – nice guy, quiet, well-mannered, except that he has a thing about suing people. He usually was suing two or three people a day, so help me. It is a known fact in town that if you hire Harry you know he's going to spend most of his time in court. He just loves to sue people and spend time with lawyers. What he does, for example, is walk down the street and wait at the bus stop for a bus. Let's say the bus stops two feet from the curb and he has to walk through a puddle of water to get on the bus. The first thing he says to the driver is, 'What is this, your stopping so far from the curb?' Bus drivers, who deal with nuts all day long, usually tell him to move his ass to the rear of the bus, and naturally, the next day he knocks out a letter to the Transit Authority informing them they're being sued for whatever crazy reason Harry thinks will work.

When he was working at Delehanty he once took on American Airlines. He had had a bad flight. He also is a racing driver, and he was on his way to a race. The flight was delayed and he missed the race. So he wrote American that he was suing. He got two beautiful vice-presidents from American as a result of that letter. They called him up and said, 'How can we settle this problem?' Harry said, 'I think the only way you can settle it is in my office and why don't you try to be here at nine-thirty in the morning?'

I didn't know what was going on but that Monday morning I needed the conference room for a meeting. I look in there and I see Harry sitting and talking with two very WASPish guys who are very disturbed. He was sitting there dictating something and a secretary was also sitting there taking it down. I had no idea what was going on, so I spotted a secretary outside the conference room and told her I needed the room for a meeting with a client. She told me that Harry's been in there for a long time and there's no sign of the meeting breaking up.

I got a little mad, but I figured he's in there with a client, although we didn't have any clients at the time who looked so beautiful. I took my client into a tiny room.

Later on that morning I asked Harry which client he had been talking to in the conference room. Harry said, 'No, that wasn't a client. Those were some guys from American

Airlines and I was dictating my terms to them. I think they're going to accept so I probably won't sue.' I said, 'You mean you took agency time as well as the conference room?' Harry said, 'Well, Jerry, it's very important to me that this thing gets straightened out.'

We fired him the next day.

Harry called me the other day asking to help get him a semiprofessional apartment. 'Harry,' I said, 'I will be glad to write anyone, anywhere, anytime, that you are indeed a semiprofessional.' 'Thank you, Jerry,' he said, and hung up, probably to sue somebody.

All the craziness doesn't stay on the creative side. The account side, which is the direct link between the agency and the client, has its madness, too. The main difference is that the creative side takes advantage of its so-called creative reputation, and guys can grow beards at the newer agencies and wear see-through shirts and pants and dilate their pupils. The account side has to stay straight and narrow and wear Paul Stuart clothes and use Ban or Secret or Right Guard and bathe once a day.

The pressure sometimes gets to the account guys, however, and when they flip out it's something beautiful to watch. I know a bunch of account guys who once had to make a trip to Batavia, Illinois, to visit the people who run the Campana Company. The Campana Company happens to be very big in the menstrual business: they make a little item called Pursettes. So here is this group of New York agency sharpies winging it in Batavia, Illinois, which, I guarantee you, is maybe one step below Des Moines. They spend the morning talking about the marketing plans of Pursettes and then they all go out to lunch. They've heard of martinis out in Batavia and the guys from New York load up – a bit too much.

Back from lunch, the president says he would like everyone around the table to sit for a while and brainstorm about other uses that Pursettes can be put to. Expand the business, explore new markets, conquer new horizons, that sort of thing. The guys from New York are sitting there in a haze and one guy pipes up, 'Hey, how about using Pursettes as torches for dwarfs?' When you're living in Batavia and you get fired by the Campana Company, there's not many other places you can go to, so the tendency in Batavia is to downplay the cracks about Pursettes. The New York guys all break up at the idea of dwarfs using Pursettes as torches, but the president of Campana frowns and everybody shuts up.

They get through the brainstorming session, and the next item on the agenda is a tour of the plant. You can't get out of Batavia without a tour of the plant. With the president leading the way, they drift through the factory and suddenly the group comes across a very strange, *very strange*-looking thing. The president proudly explains that this *thing* is an artificial vagina, in fact its name is the syngina, and naturally, it tests how good Pursettes are. The guys from New York are looking at these synginas and they're biting through their lips to keep from laughing. The president keeps carrying on about how good these synginas are and finally one New Yorker says, 'And if you're real nice, they let you take the syngina to dinner.' Here are guys collapsing on the floor of a factory in Batavia, Illinois, the president turning white with rage, the advertising manager petrified with fear, the agency guys still too stoned to worry.

I once worked for a vice-president of an agency whom we called The Klutz. The Klutz always managed to sit through a presentation and screw it up at the end. We used to make a book on when he would open his mouth and blow the pitch.

We kept telling him – his name was David – 'Please stay away from the presentations if you can't stop insulting people.' David would say, 'I'm going to behave, I'm really going to be a nice guy.' He had this awful tendency to insult the client and he was truly dangerous to have around.

One day we're pitching for the Tourist Bureau of Mexico account and the bagman for President Alemán of Mexico shows up to hear the pitch. The idea was if you got your pitch past the bagman, then you got to pitch to the top tamale himself. The pitch went on for a hell of a long time, something like two hours, and David was a marvel. He sat there, not saying a word, and I was beginning to feel sorry about the way we yelled at him. 'He's great,' I said to myself, 'he's behaving like a real gent. I'm sorry we bugged him before the meeting about his behavior.'

For two hours he was beautiful. The meeting ends and I say to myself, 'Thank God, we made it, the meeting's over and he hasn't blown it, he hasn't insulted the guy, he hasn't done anything.' So David puts his arm around the bagman, whose name may have been Pedro or José or whatever, and as they're walking out the door – *out the door* – David says, 'Pedro, you're a nice guy. We're going to be working together, I'm sure, and you'll see we're nice people, too. If you keep up the niceness, José, maybe we'll give you back Texas.' I knew right then and there we were dead.

Because there is so much craziness in advertising, you live for great lines. A funny line literally helps you get through the day. One of the best lines I ever heard was thrown when I was at Delehanty, Kurnit & Geller. We were making a pitch to the American Enka Company, which was run by a beautiful blond George Macready type, the kind who was on the other side in World War II movies. Making the pitch was Shep Kurnit, the president of the agency, Marvin Davis, a vice-president, a guy named Tully Plesser, who is a market-research man, and a couple of others, including me. Without getting too ethnic, the faces were basic Jewish and Italian. The pitch went well, Kurnit and Davis were fine, and then the blond guy retired from the room to discuss the agency with some of his people. He walked back in and said, 'The account is yours if you can produce Delehanty.'

CHAPTER FIVE
DANCING IN THE DARK

'What account guys have to do to survive today is dance. By dancing, I mean they've got to be agile, with very, very good footwork so they don't get shot down easily. You see, they've got nothing to sell. Your copywriter, no matter how young or how bad, has his book – his portfolio – to show. An art director also has a portfolio. Or they've got reels, short presentations containing all the commercials they've ever shot. But what does the account man have to show? Nothing . . .'

The people I sympathize most with in advertising are the account guys – the fellows who are the middlemen between the creative troops and the client. Account guys have to put up with the craziness of the creative people, work out marketing and campaign plans, and then sell the package to the client. Under the best circumstances, it isn't easy. Here is your clean-cut account guy, mortgaged up to his ears in Chappaqua, trying to deal with a zonked kid writer who is maybe twenty-three or twenty-four and is living in a loft in the East Village with twelve other acidheads. The account guy has to get the ad out of the kid and then sell it to the client, who is pretty tough himself. There are a lot of guys crying themselves to sleep up there in old Chappaqua because they're caught in the crazy middle.

The Hucksters wasn't all that far from the truth. It's been written up that the Lucky Strike account, when George Washington Hill was acting every bit as bad as Sidney Greenstreet, had something like twenty-one account supervisors on it in a two-year period. During that time some six or seven guys had heart attacks, several had cases of nervous exhaustion, and the last guy had a complete breakdown. Then in came Fairfax Cone, young, tough, bright, and takes over the account and holds it and solidifies it and becomes The Man, you know? And then Frederick Wakeman writes a book about it, except in the book the guy goes into Sulka, I think, and spends his last twenty dollars or so on a sincere tie. I assure you no sincere tie ever made any impression on George Washington Hill.

What account guys have to do to survive today is dance. By dancing, I mean they've got to be agile, with very, very good footwork so they don't get shot down easily. You see, they've got nothing to sell. Your copywriter, no matter how young or how bad, has his book – his portfolio – to show. An art director also has a portfolio. Or they've got reels, short presentations containing all the commercials they've ever shot. But what does the account man have to show? Nothing.

What's going on in advertising today – the real revolution – is that the younger agencies, the Mary Wellses, the Doyle, Danes, the Carl Allys, eliminate jobs. This is what is causing the upheaval on Madison Avenue. Every time you read of an account moving from an older agency like Foote, Cone & Belding, Compton, or Lennen & Newell to one of the newer and smaller agencies, jobs are eliminated. And account men are affected most of all in these moves.

Let's take TWA when it was at Foote, Cone. Here is an account billing about $22 million a year, and although I don't know the exact figures I'd be willing to bet there were about seventy-five people having something to do with the account. Again, I don't know how many people Mary Wells has on the account, but I'd be willing to bet it's a hell of a lot fewer people – maybe no more than fifty people. And doing a good job. The point is, you don't need twelve guys servicing TWA and holding their hands and fifteen guys running around wondering if their coffee is warm enough and what they can do. A Mary Wells eliminates jobs. She produces good advertising which is what the game is all about, so she doesn't need account guys jumping out of their skins every time somebody from TWA calls the office.

Let's take TWA one step farther. As a hypothetical example, let's figure TWA moves out of Wells to Daniel & Charles. I don't think Danny Karsch would have fifty people working on the account. I'd estimate that he would get by by using maybe thirty or thirty-five people: four copy and art people, two promotion copy and art, three or four in media, two or three in research, three in marketing, three in production, and then secretaries and bookkeeping people. So, from an original one hundred people you're down to maybe thirty-five. And there are sixty-five people on the beach. What I'm getting at is that the number of people working on an account is in direct relationship to the quality of the work being turned out. If you can find four great writers and four great art directors, you can have yourself a fantastic campaign. And let TWA worry about its own hot coffee.

There's a very good account in town in terms of the prestige attached to it. The billing is nothing, but the prestige is terrific. This account has been with an old-line agency for almost fifty years. Well, the grandson of the founder of the business is comparatively young, maybe forty-two or forty-three, and he has come to the conclusion that maybe the people at this old-line agency don't understand his problems. Now after fifty years, this is the equivalent of a guy going to his wife and saying, 'Tootsie, I want a divorce.'

The wife, sitting there with her fifty-year-old varicose veins, says, 'Divorce?' And the guy says, 'Yeah, it's very strange. I want a divorce to marry a young chick who's about seventeen years old and who's making a lot of noise. Right now she's about to be arrested for running nude down Madison Avenue. You know, I realize that we've lived together for a long time and you've done an awful lot for me and we've grown up together, but I want a divorce. I mean, I see something down the block that's really fantastic. I want to try it.'

You can see the desperation that's going on in the older agencies. They rant and rave at agencies like mine, like Leber, Katz, Paccione, Carl Ally, Delehanty, all the newer agencies, even Doyle, Dane, which is only twenty or so years old. In a sense guys are coming to the older agencies and asking for divorces, and then they're running out with these young chicks. And so what the older agencies do is try to act like a woman who is trying to hold onto her husband. Like a fifty-year-old woman hanging onto the breadwinner. The older agencies go out and buy a load of cosmetics and eye shadow and they put all this stuff on and do their hair – this is what they're doing when they start hiring freaky young kids at star salaries. This is the façade, they're putting on all this stuff and saying, 'Well, if this is what it takes to hold my guy I'll just hold my nose and do it.' But they wind up looking like a fifty-year-old lady who's wearing a miniskirt and dressed like a kid. They can't make it that way, but they try, and the try costs them a lot of bread.

The agency president who has just lost an account worth a million dollars to his agency is not going to be the friendly, warm guy who the day before thought he had that million dollars locked in, and he's going to transmit his feelings to his creative staff, right down to the account people. The account people know what to do – tranquilizers or aspirin. Big aspirin-takers in the advertising business. Advertising is a fantastic source of revenue to the aspirin business. Librium, Miltown – but heavy on the aspirin.

I've worked with guys who just pop aspirin as though they were going out of their minds. They have headaches, that lousy feeling – they don't know what it is – and they sit there and pop aspirin all day long. In turn, they sell aspirin. When I was up at Bates, we probably sold more aspirin for the Anacin account than any other agency in the United States in the aspirin business, and we also consumed more Anacin than any other agency, too.

A good example of having that uneasy feeling is now taking place over at Foote, Cone. Now they're a very good, very big agency that has been having tough luck and there's uneasiness all over that place. I know, because I'm talking to account executives from there. Doors are kept closed all day long. Everybody has their door closed. The account guys don't come out in the halls. That's where the shrapnel is. Guys sit in their offices. And it becomes boring. It becomes tiring. You want to go to sleep. Your arms are tired. So are your legs. A boredom factor sets in at any large agency when the luck is going bad and when everything tastes a little rotten. There's a lot of yawning and people can't quite get with it. Guys are walking around saying, 'Ah, what the hell, this is a lousy business and I think I'm going to get out of it.'

There is a physical change in an agency when the business starts to go. I saw it at Fuller & Smith & Ross when they were starting to blow business. Not only were guys logy – they actually started to get sick. Guys stay out with a bad back. They start to walk slower. Sometimes you really don't know quite what's wrong with them, but they're not healthy any more. At Bates the guys took Anacin.

What a wonderful thing for the economists to play with. There's a great case of an agency taking its product seriously.

Some of the biggest aspirin-takers that I've met in advertising are the hip-pocket account guys. Hip-pocket guys are a dying breed, but while they hang on they're wonderful to watch. A hip-pocket guy has an account in his pocket. Account guys are able to get employment contracts at agencies if they come in with pocket business. A guy with pocket business can deliver the account – he's in so tight with the account for whatever reason that he owns it, it's his, nobody can touch it. Someplace along the line he impressed the account enough so that they'll stick with this guy for life if he just plays along. There's a guy in town who represents an entire industry – let's call it the peacock-feather industry. All the breeders of peacocks got together and formed a Peacock Feather Breeders' Association to do national advertising, lobbying, and whatever.

This fellow, Al, has been working with the Peacock Feather people for years. The Peacock Feather Breeders' Association wouldn't make any kind of advertising move whatever without Al's being involved. When Al started working with the Peacock Feather account it was worth $1,000,000 in billing a year. Because the demand for peacock feathers has not been what it used to be – ladies don't wear hats any more and so on – the account today bills only $300,000 a year. And Al has been moving the account around. It's been to at least three agencies that I know of.

Now it may seem that the account is vanishing right before your eyes, but take a look at the economics involved. The account is still attractive enough to agencies in town so that if Al ever lets the word out that he – and the Peacock Feather Breeders' Association – are available, he'll get fifty calls, I guarantee you. Wherever he goes, he can say, 'I've three hundred thousand dollars' worth of business.' Figure that an average agency could make $45,000 on that billing in commissions and another $15,000 in production charges. So an agency could make $60,000 a year on a guy by the name of Al. Let's also say that Al goes for $35,000 a year in salary, so the agency now has Al paying for himself plus maybe $20,000 or $25,000 left over. Plus, they've got Al around most of the time to work on three or four other accounts, which is also free of charge, plus whatever he can go out and pitch. They've got it knocked. He's worth it to them. Except that they don't realize what he costs their creative image, which is considerable. Because whatever the president of the Peacock Feather Breeders' Association wants, Al has to deliver. Otherwise he can't live, he can't hold the account. So he screws up their image, and that's what is essentially wrong with hip-pocket accounts.

How does a client get locked into a guy like Al? The client goes to the theater once too often with Al. He wins a game of golf from Al once too often. The client really starts to believe that Al is a good advertising man. Somewhere between the escargots and the baked Alaska the client starts to think Al is God. The client is not so smart in some of these cases. In other cases it's like absentee management. Very interesting. It's like the real top management isn't around, so the guy who *is* in charge of spending the money gets into bed with another guy. And I don't think there are kickbacks involved here, either. Just bad judgment.

There is a cheese account in town – let's call it French Cheese – and it must bill $1,000,000 a year. French Cheese's top management is in Paris. They know nothing. The people running French Cheese in New York don't know much more than the French do about advertising, but they do trust an account guy named Jimmy. Jimmy, in fact, has French Cheese stuck way deep into his pocket. He's moved the account to at least four agencies. Jimmy, of course, has to remain very, very friendly with the French Cheese guy here. They go to the theater a lot. Their wives are friends – and they better be friends because Jimmy lives or dies for this account. This account means $80,000 a year to Jimmy and Mrs. Jimmy, plus a Caddie and a couple of other things thrown in. So every year, as long as Jimmy remains friendly with the French Cheese guy in New York, he's got his eighty grand. But he has to perform, no question about that. So long as he does, the account is locked. No agency could pitch that account without having Jimmy on their payroll.

Let me make it clear – hip-pocket business goes on way beyond Jimmy and his French Cheese. Guys get to be presidents of agencies because they have business locked in. You control a certain amount of business, and then you muscle. You've got more clout than the next guy. At one agency where I worked it was very simple. One guy played golf with a guy who controlled the advertising for a very big automobile account. Another guy had a lock on an enormous piece of cigarette business – *but not so big as the automobile business*. Very simple. The guy controlling the automobile business told the guy controlling the tobacco business that he wanted to be chairman of the board. And he was. The other guy settled for being president.

When I went to work at Ted Bates, I was told you can screw around with the entire place, but don't touch this particular guy. He is so close to the Fleischmann booze business that if he ever gets angry, we're in trouble. The entire agency was afraid of this guy. He had his own office, his own secretary, and he never had much to do. He was pulling down fifty grand a year and the word was, 'He's got the Fleischmann account in his pocket.' He supposedly played golf with the advertising manager and the rumor always was: 'He's the guy who's going to take the account with him if he ever leaves Bates.' Everybody was terrorized by this guy, and the funny thing was he was a lovely guy, a great guy who never shoved anyone around, never raised his voice.

There must have been a good two hundred people – account executives, copywriters, art directors, and so forth – walking very quietly around this guy. Right down the line, one after the other, we knew we must not screw around with this guy. Not only was he making big bucks, he put in a big expense account each year. He did everything he wanted, had people hired, had people fired, did the whole thing. Well, it lasted a year and a half or so. But while he lasted he was class all the way.

They finally said to themselves, 'His expense account is going to put us out of business.' That's how far he was going – he was literally taking money out of their pockets to the point where the account was no longer going to be profitable if they didn't put a stop to it. So they took a calculated risk, fear and all, and they decided they were going to fire the guy.

The day they fired him they found out something – the whole thing was a myth. He had no control over the account, had no lock on the business. The guy had gotten his job based on the rumor that they were going to lose the account but if they hired this guy they'd save the account. In fact, the rumor was all over town. So they hired him – and then they fired him. It's a beautiful story because if the guy hadn't run up such a big expense account he'd still be there. They still have the account, by the way. The guy walked out of there and started his own agency, and for weeks the rumor around Bates was that he was going to take the Fleischmann business with him. It never happened.

What's sad about the advertising business is that I could take anyone with the proper number of ears, eyes, arms, and so forth, and land him a job at any agency in the city on the theory of pocket business. I would say that your grandmother is a relative of someone who controls a lot of business and then you're in for at least a year, maybe more.

When Bates lost Mobil Gas to Doyle, Dane, Bernbach, their first line was, 'We got to keep the top guys who used to be on this account simply because we're going to attract another gas company. We can land another gasoline if we have these people around. But the other guys [the little people] have to go because they don't mean anything – we can't parade them out.'

One of the gas guys was moved over and put on the Wink business. The gag around the agency was that maybe Wink doesn't taste that much different from gasoline. They had still another guy who was their real gas *maven*. No one really quite figured out what he was doing until he quit. For years they kept this guy in his office, and he was always full of great plans. He was always pitching an account that he was very close to because he went to school with somebody. If I wanted to start all over again and people didn't know what I looked like, I could go into practically any agency and hint that I'm very tight and close to a lot of business and live there for two or three years. They don't fire you once they think you're close to business.

Once, many years ago, I went looking for work at Sullivan, Stauffer, Colwell & Bayles. In those days it was a very, very nervous agency. I asked to do an assignment and met a copy group chief. The conversation went something like this: 'I'd like to do an assignment just to show you that I can work for you. I obviously haven't got any samples in my portfolio.' He said, 'Well, I like the rough samples you have, and I'm going to give you an assignment. I want you to do something on Rinso. Oh, no. Wait a minute. Rinso might hear that we're giving out assignments and there might be some word around that we're in trouble on Rinso. Why don't you do it on Bulova? No! Bulova is very touchy now, and there's a little political situation.' And he's talking to a guy who wanted ninety bucks a week, who knew no one in the business. Finally, he couldn't give me an assignment.

An agency president once told me, 'I start worrying about losing an account the minute I get it. The minute I sign the contract, I'm one step closer toward losing it.' At that point he's worried and his contribution to the advertising is fear. He pushes it to the people under him: 'We've got to hold, we've got to hold.' A good example of this is Yardley, which came into Bates while I was there, and at the first meeting the word was, 'We want great work, we want creative work.' Terrific! Everyone shook hands, and we opened up the booze for special occasions and had a party.

The next day – I swear, the *next* day – the word was out: 'We're in danger of losing the account. We've got to be very careful of the way we handle it.' So work was done and never shown to the client. Why? 'We can't afford to show him stuff like this right now.' Step one: fear. They're afraid to even show him work. So they show him what they consider safe. And safe is not what he came to the agency for.

I felt like a shill in the Yardley pitch. They trotted me out and showed the Yardley people some of the work that I had done on Pretty Feet while I was at Delehanty, Kurnit & Geller. And Yardley was sold a bill of goods that I was going to be in charge of the account. All I ever did was work on one piece of the account and then the agency never wanted to show the work to the client. The people were afraid of the work and didn't even want to let the client say no to it. So they did some off-the-wall garbage and they showed it to the client and the client threw it back in their laps. I mean, it was real garbage. And they were hung. The account moved from Bates to Delehanty. Delehanty resigned it when they picked up Coty, which conflicted with Yardley. Yardley then started its own house agency and recently gave that up for Benton & Bowles and Davis, Parker and Valenti.

Accounts move around so much these days because they're not getting what they want. It's the agency's job to express what they need. That's the agency's job. The client simply knows where he wants his product to go in the marketplace. My agency just picked up a new account and the client said, 'I've had two agencies, one which insisted that everything they did was gold and I got rid of them, and the other agency which came in every day and said, "What would you like to see on paper this week?" ' My partner Ron Travisano puts it another way: 'Would you like to see something in an open-toe campaign?' An account shouldn't be treated that way. He should be guided, but he shouldn't be forced into doing anything he really doesn't want to do.

Most account guys live with fear in their hearts. I know a guy in town named Coolidge. He once was very big at an agency called Cunningham & Walsh. Big money. Maybe ninety big ones a year. He got fired from there and thanks to his good friend, Beautiful Jim, at Fuller & Smith & Ross, he zipped over to Fuller & Smith as a creative supervisor. Coolidge lives in Westport, knows the right people, he's very soft-spoken, does none of the things that people assume an agency guy would do. But he doesn't live like a human being. He's got that fear crawling in him every day. Most of these guys start the day off deciding which account is going to call them and scare them. All an account has to do to terrorize an account man is call up and say, 'Hey, can you send me some copies of the last five ads you've done for us?' and the panic spreads.

Yet this doesn't go on at Doyle, Dane. They never think they're going to lose anything. They've got a marvelous track record and they're confident. Mary Wells isn't sitting there worrying about whether she's going to lose anything. And she usually doesn't. I'm convinced of this.

Sometimes the creative people get sucked into becoming shills. Let's say a guy is doing a terrific job on a cosmetic account for a small agency. Let's say further that an old-line agency has a cosmetic account that is in trouble. So, there's big fear going around. The big agency will decide to sandbag. They go out and pull in stars and offer them fantastic salaries. Who can resist? Maybe the star copywriter would like to move the hell out of the East Village and breathe some of that good Westport air. So they can't resist. They show up and they work on the pitch to save the account. The agency was doomed to lose the account anyway. The account goes, the guy goes. He was led into a trap and slaughtered. There have been many cases of this sort of thing and it's very, very bad business.

Creative people don't have a business sense about themselves. When I went to work at Bates I had one of the first contracts in the history of the Bates creative department. No one had ever asked for one. And they've had hundreds and hundreds of people go in and out of that creative department. Creative people don't consider what can happen. Most creative people don't know their own pattern of work and they aren't smart enough – quite honestly – to go in and say, 'I want a contract.' I asked for and got a specific type of contract. I wanted it for eighteen months – not two years, or a year, but eighteen months. I told them that after four months they were going to hate me, and I meant *despise* me. 'You won't be able to stand me,' I told them. 'And after another eight months, you're going to start grudgingly to like me but you would have fired me months ago if I didn't have that contract. And after that I'm going to score. If I can make it for eighteen months, I'll stay for life. If I don't make it. I'll pull out.' Which is what I did. When I was at Delehanty for only four months Shep Kurnit was out looking for a new creative director. I stayed there for two and a half years.

I find it easy to hire an art director or a copywriter, but when an account executive comes in to see me I don't even know what to ask him. I go through a session with this guy and spend most of the time reading my shoelaces. I have nothing to tell the guy, nothing to ask him. Should I ask him how he smiles? Should I ask him how do you handle yourself with clients? 'Oh, I handle myself very well.' 'Waiter, how's the liver tonight?' 'Oh, the liver's terrific today.' How the hell does the waiter know? How the hell do I know if the account guy is good with the account?

'What accounts have you worked on?' 'Well, when I was on General Foods, I kept us from losing the account for nine months.' General Foods has hundreds of guys on the account. And this guy kept the account for nine months! Maybe he did. I don't know. Not long ago I had two guys in my office who were from the same agency and had worked on the same account. The first guy came in and said, 'When I was on the account, I helped them introduce "soft gin."' Two hours later, so help me, another guy walks in and says, 'I was the fellow who introduced "soft gin."' Now, if one of those cats wasn't lying, then they were identical twins. And they both said they were account supervisors on the account.

When I talked to the two 'soft gin' guys, I was in the market for two account men. I had seen maybe thirty-five guys, and twenty of them were out of work. All right, there are twenty guys looking for a job, and I've got room for only two. They've all had jobs. Once they were important guys in some agency. Once they were the guys who really did the 'soft gin' marketing plan. They lost their jobs, and all of a sudden they have no value at all, except for a guy who might need an account man for a liquor account. Now I was looking for a wine guy, and the two 'soft gin' guys know only gin, they don't know from wine. It is much easier for an agency to hire an account man who knows a piece of business. He can jump right in and start working; you don't have to teach him. When you have a choice, you take a guy with experience.

I meet these account people on the street and I meet more people out of work than those who are working. A lot of them just don't stick to the business. A lot of them just can't come back. They're too specialized. The jobs are disappearing and the business is changing. Some of them go into the real-estate business; other guys go into the graphic-arts business. Maybe they buy a boat and sail away. They just can't make it. They can't take the feast-or-famine aspect of the business. It's not romantic or glamorous, it's tragic.

The average age of the account executive is thirty-two, thirty-three, and then they start lying about their age. I had a guy in my office who was gray. My God, I practically had to help him out the door. He claimed he was thirty-eight. Well, if he was thirty-eight he's lived a great life. I mean, he really looked like he was in his early fifties. I mean, the guy was an old man.

Guys are out of work a long time, and they start to lie about their age, and that, too, is part of the fear. Good people are out of work, not just losers. This is one of the few businesses where you can be out of work and tell the world. In most other lines of work, usually you hide and don't tell your neighbors you're on the beach. If a guy gets fired, he gets on the phone and calls the first twenty people he can think of. And it's all over town that he's been fired. The kids are killing a lot of account people, too. A lot of hard-working young kids are now willing to take a crack at account work. Agencies that used to start kids in the mailroom are taking more chances and giving kids accounts after a couple of years at the agency.

In the old days it was a slow process out of the mailroom to account work.

When a guy is out, he tries anything. He becomes a consultant – that's the first step. He tries to get all of his friends to give him consultation work. He might look to the magazines as a space salesman. He might turn up working for a printing outfit. The average account man starts making plans to start his own agency after he's fired. He says, 'Well, screw them all. I was going to start my own agency anyway.' But that doesn't work out. He can't get the bread. The account he thought he had sewn up wasn't sewn up. He's not connected anywhere, and slowly he starts to find that he's got nine or twelve months of debts ahead of him. The guy is going to be looking for a new job for at least a year. There's no wonder that an account man is afraid, knowing that if he goes, he's going to be out this long. It's natural. You've got to be afraid. You spend every day knowing that if you blow it, you're out for a year. That's what the average guy spends on the beach today. The shrinking job market is making it tough as hell for people to find a new job quickly.

And nobody has that kind of money in the bank. The worst story I ever heard along these lines wasn't about an account man but a copywriter. He had been a star, and he came to see me about a job. He was in his late fifties. His portfolio was complete with samples, but they were at least eight years old. I said, 'How long have you been out of work?' He said it had been something like six or seven years, he wasn't quite sure at that point. I said, 'How in God's name did you survive?' He said, 'Well, I sold the house in Darien. I sold all my stocks – and I had quite a few of them. I sold some real estate for a while and my wife and I moved to a small apartment in Brooklyn.' He was working his way backwards. Six or seven years went by without a permanent job, no office to go into in the morning. The guy had no real income for all that time. He was begging me for some freelance work. He wanted a day's work. Here is a guy who was once earning $30,000 to $40,000 a year. When they fall, they fall very hard, and everyone – account guys and creative people – knows that the fall down is very tough. We're in a business that is very fashion-conscious. I mean, what's in style this year may not be salable next year. The guy with talent from one era has a tough time adjusting to the new style.

One of the 'soft gin' guys who came to see me had been out of work for only a few days, but really he had been out for six months. He knew his agency was going to lose the account six months before. So he's had six months of looking for a job. Age fifty-two. Chances, zip. Who's going to hire him? He hints around that. 'I may have some business.' He doesn't have any business. If he had business, he would have kept it. He would have used the business to keep his job.

With the creative guys becoming more important, the account guys are having a tougher time of it. The entire structure of advertising is being disturbed. I get an account, and somebody loses a job someplace. In the large, older agencies many account executives work on only one account. In the smaller agencies one account man services several accounts. We have a handful of account executives servicing a couple of dozen accounts. That means there are a lot of account executives who are out of work because of us. For some people this could be a terrifying business, with good reason.

I've never been frightened because I always had something to show. I had something I knew how to do – copywriting. And I know what it's like to be poor. I really know what it's like to be broke. It's not that terrifying. It's not that bad, it's not the end of the world. Christ, I was born in Brooklyn and I was living there up until a few years ago. I know how to get on the train and go back there. The Transit Authority has got pretty good signs showing you how to get to Brooklyn.

Part of the problem, especially with the account guys, is that they are living way over their heads. Advertising is a business that goes first class all the way. When you get hooked on the expense-account way of life, there's a tendency to try to live out of the office the way you do in the office. This is part of it. They own boats, they belong to yacht clubs, they live in expensive houses. A lot of these guys are living very close to the edge. I would bet that most of them haven't got any money in the bank. No bucks salted away. They just about make it. And they live very high indeed.

They're living on loans. They've got big liquor bills. Big partying bills. Big school bills for the kids. Big clothes bills. Big everything. The nut is very high for these cats. That house in Rye – they've got to live in Rye – has got to cost them seventy-five big ones. And when you've got a seventy-five-grand house with a mortgage this big, you don't answer the client back that fast. You know, you're not too quick to screw around. You're not too ready to do anything except pop a lot of pills and maybe run up a big bill with the shrink.

The account man is in the only business in the world where he gets hired, is paid a lot of money for four or five years, and then at one point he's told he's not worth anything any more because they've lost the account. You know, if you go into any other business in the world and you last five years or so you're going to live there forever. You go to work in this business and if you last for five years the chances are you're going to be fired the next day. Seniority means nothing. This is not the railroads. There's too much money at stake. These guys know what happens when they lose a job. They've got no place to go for a year or so. I mean, they can't send their wife out to work, they're past all that.

It hits everybody in the business, not just the account executives. I know a very good art director who's been out of work for eleven months. And he's good, in fact he just won an award at a show. The guy is fantastic. He was making $40,000 a year but now he says he'll 'negotiate.' That means $25,000 a year. He's making too much money. I could get some crazy kid to come in and start at $7,000 a year and keep raising him up and up and after five or six years, if I could hang on to him that long, you couldn't hire an equivalent art director for $50,000. I've got one art director who's twenty-two, and I just hired an eighteen-year-old. The twenty-two-year-old is like an old man next to the eighteen-year-old, who really is far out. These kids are cheaper, they work harder, they're less problem. It's a matter of simple economics. And they show: out of schools, off the streets, out of the woodwork. God knows where they come from. It's the kids who are really revolutionizing the advertising business today. It's the kids with nothing to lose. The kids are pushing ahead, mainly because they communicate to consumers like we've never communicated before. In a couple of years 50 percent of the population is going to be under the age of twenty-five. When we reach this point the kids in advertising are going to take over completely.

CHAPTER SIX
THE CREATIVE LIFE

'Now advertising is a small business, with a lot of gossip, and there are a lot of guys sitting around in their offices with not too much to do, so when they hear a funny story or a crazy line they sit and call each other up to pass it on. I became known as the Pearl Harbor guy at Panasonic . . .'

There are talented people all over New York today who are capable of turning out advertising that doesn't drive people crazy and does sell the product. Problem is whether the people can sell their advertising to their agencies and their accounts. Within every big agency there's a pocket of good people who for some reason manage to save the situation, make the advertising and do it well. Within every agency. When I went to Bates my team was, I modestly believe, that quality pocket of advertising. We turned out some excellent advertising at Bates. In one year, we literally turned the Panasonic Electronics account around.

It took some doing. My title was Creative Supervisor when I went to Bates. But I was part of the zoo. Bates had to form a zoo so that they could take their clients to it and show me to them: 'Hey, look, he's creative, he's won awards, he dresses funny, he does all those mystical things that you hear about.' What they were saying was: 'Like we're in on it, we know exactly what it's all about. Don't worry, baby, you're going to get the same kind of work that you've been reading about other people getting.' Somebody once described it as Operation Judas Goat. I was supposed to come in there and pull in a lot of people from the outside. The idea was that other writers and art directors would look at me and say, 'Gee, if Della Femina is going in there, maybe it's worthwhile. Maybe I ought to take a shot at it and forget all about those crazy hammers inside people's skulls pushing aspirin.' I had something of a reputation among creative people in town for doing good work. At that point they might want to try a place like Bates. So the notion was that hiring me was going to upgrade their entire image. This is the way they planned it. It was not the way I planned it. The first thing I decided to do was to make a declaration of my intentions, sort of to say, 'Look, this is what it's going to be like and I'm not going to put up with most of the pompous crap that goes through the agency.'

The first day they had a meeting on the Japanese electronics company, Panasonic, and there must have been six or seven guys there: the account supervisor, the account executive, the executive art director, and a couple of others. I figured I'd keep my mouth shut for a few minutes, like it was my first morning in the place. One guy said, 'Well, what are we going to do about Panasonic?' And everybody sat around, frowning and thinking about Panasonic. Finally, I decided, what the hell, I'll throw a line to loosen them up – I mean, they were paying me $50,000 a year plus a $5,000-a-year expense account, and I thought they deserved something for all this bread. So I said, 'Hey, I've got it, I've got it.' Everbody jumped. Then I got very dramatic, really setting them up. 'I see a headline, yes, I see this headline.' 'What is it?' they yelled. 'I see it all now,' I said, 'I see an entire campaign built around this headline.' They all were looking at me now. 'The headline is, the headline is: "From Those Wonderful Folks Who Gave You Pearl Harbor."'

Complete silence. Dead silence. And then the art director went into hysterics, like he was hitting the floor. To him it was funny. One of the account guys who was smoking a pipe – well, his mouth opened up at the line and his pipe dropped all over him, and he spent the next five minutes trying to put out the sparks. The rest of them looked at me as if to say, 'God, where are we, what did we do?' They looked very depressed. I was pretty pleased. I thought it wasn't too bad a line. Later in the day I repeated the line to the guy who hired me, did the same bit for him. The feeling wasn't spontaneous as all that the second time around but it served its purpose. I know why I do these things: it sets the pace, it really tells people who I am, what I feel.

Now advertising is a small business, with a lot of gossip, and there are a lot of guys sitting around in their offices with not too much to do, so when they hear a funny story or a crazy line they sit and call each other up to pass it on. I became known as the Pearl Harbor guy at Panasonic.

I wouldn't say that things went downhill for me at the agency after that first meeting. It really started to go to hell at Bates after my first creative review board meeting. One of the reasons that copywriters and art directors go crazy is creative review boards. Creative review boards are, first of all, the device of a very large and a very old-fashioned agency. It's made up so a lot of guys who are over sixty can feel as though they're part of an agency. A lot of these guys, they have nothing to do and they sit there. They're professional second-guessers, and they sit there and they want the chance to review the creative product. If somebody were to ask me what are the physical characteristics of a creative review board, I would say they are made up of guys with red noses and blue veins. And like they sit there and they look like they're just about to have a coronary. They have this beautiful flush, most of them are gray and they're maybe twenty to thirty pounds overweight. These are the guys who have survived to the point where they now make seventy-five, eighty, one hundred grand a year without doing very much. They show up at the office at 10:00 a.m. Maybe. They spend a couple of hours shuffling papers around on the desk and calling people up and making their lunch dates. They're very concerned with their lunch dates. God forbid they should ever get caught without a lunch date. They wouldn't know what to do. They make their lunch date. They show up at

'21,' which is the place they all go to, and they spend another two or three hours a day there at lunch.

They never talk about advertising. That's a funny thing. These cats talk about advertising *only* at creative review board meetings. They get back to their offices around three o'clock and maybe they'll call a meeting for no good reason and comes 4:45 they grab the train and go back to Rye or Chappaqua where they all live. They all live in the same valley as far as I'm concerned – the Valley of Death. Man for man, creative review boards are probably responsible for more waste in advertising than anything else. The Comptons have them, and the Thompsons, and the Bateses, and the Foote, Cones, and the Fuller, Smiths and just about every one of those old-line, heavy, overstaffed, fat agencies. The joke of the business is that an agency like a Compton has a creative review board. So they get together once a month, these killers, and they review.

Why should a Mary Wells have a creative review board, or a Doyle, Dane, or a Delehanty? They *know* they're good, they don't need any board to tell themselves so. The evidence is in their fantastic growth and in the awards they win each year for their work. I don't believe that people should have their writing reviewed.

Now the creative review board at Bates was a new deal. Bates hadn't had one before. A first for them. And to their credit I must say that they had some younger people in it. It wasn't just the red noses and the blue veins. With one or two exceptions, they had some very young, very untalented people whom they put on the board. It's amazing how you could be that young and that untalented.

I had been at Bates for five or six months when the word got out that I was going to be the first guy reviewed by their new creative review board. And that bugged me. After they told me that I was it, I said, 'O.K. Here are my golden rules. I will not defend anything that I have done. All I will do is show you what I have done and answer your questions. I'm not here to defend myself.'

I did have stuff to show. I had the Panasonic, I had Royal Globe Insurance, which was doing pretty well, and I had some other things that my group had produced. The Royal Globe television commercial we had done was very dramatic. The viewer was put in the driver's seat – at night – and for sixty seconds all you saw were blinding headlights. We were a group. They used us like a special squad to be brought in whenever something went wrong. Whenever somebody was about to lose an account, whenever there was a new business pitch, my group – Ron Travisano, Frank Siebke, Ned Tolmach and I – would be called in. But Bates was getting a little uptight about the group and they were looking forward to their creative review board session.

The night before the meeting I really didn't know what to do. I was sitting at home saying to myself, 'I've got to do something, I've got to find a way to show them exactly what I think of the meeting.' And then it hit me. I'd walk in there with a tape recorder and tape the entire proceedings.

I showed up the next day to face the board, which was made up of about seven guys, whose average salary was maybe $80,000 a year. One guy there, the Creative Director of the World – that was his title and it meant Creative Director of the Bates World – was making maybe $120,000. The other guys weighed in at $80,000 and $90,000, and there were a couple of lower-echelon guys able to grab off only $70,000 a year. I was by far the lowest-paid guy in the place. I mean, there must have been close to a half-million dollars a year in salary there.

As I walked in, one guy had to be a wise guy and throw a line: 'Well, have you got the crown of thorns ready for him?' And they all laughed. Then I put the little tape recorder down on the table. They quit laughing and immediately all eyes just went to the thing. I said, 'I've got my ads pinned up and like I said before if you have any questions about the quality or type of advertising I'll be happy to answer anything you want. But before we do that I would like to turn on the tape recorder and record this session.' Before I turned it on I said, 'If there's anyone in this room who objects to being taped I'll be very happy to leave it off.' And everyone just kind of shuffled and said nothing. So I turned it on and said, 'O.K., let's have some questions.'

Nothing. One guy cleared his throat and hemmed and hawed, and said, 'Well, I notice you use a black background on that ad for Royal Globe.' All the while he's watching that Concord tape recorder work. It wasn't even a Panasonic recorder. I said, 'That's right, we felt a black background would be better.' More nothing. And then babble, pure babble, all babble. Two solid hours of babbling. They were terrified, and I know it, and it's beautiful, and I'm sitting there and talking and just answering any question they want, but they're not asking any questions. One guy talks about pro football. Guys start talking about anything they could think of and all the while they're staring at the machine, they couldn't keep their eyes off that machine. Ned Tolmach, who was sitting next to me during the entire meeting, was watching this whole beautiful scene with amazement.

And finally, after two hours of nonsense, I said, 'You know, gentlemen, I don't think there is anything else that you want to ask me, is there?' They're still looking and one of them says, 'No.' So I shut the tape recorder off and I say, 'Well, thank you,' and we walk out. As Ned and I walked out of the room I turned to him and said, 'Ned, do you think it worked?' Ned said, 'I don't know if it worked, but boy, are they fucking stupid people up here.' 'Could it be that they're just stupid?' I asked. 'I don't know,' he said, 'I just can't figure it.'

As I was walking down the hall and approaching my office I could hear the telephone ringing. I broke into a run and grabbed the phone and it's the $120,000-a-year Creative Director of the World. 'Jerry,' he says on the phone, 'can you come down to my office and bring that tape recorder?' And I said, 'Bring in my tape recorder?' 'And bring the tape, too.' I said, 'But there's nothing on the tape. It's useless to me now. But I'll run it over again if you want.' 'Just bring the tape, Jerry.'

On my way to the Creative Director of the World's office I met four of the guys in the hall who were in that creative review board meeting. One of the $75,000-a-year biggies – I'll call him Kent – is standing right there in the hallway, blocking my way, and he's looking even more nervous than he usually looked, which was pretty nervous anyhow. 'Jerry,' Kent said, 'why'd you bring that tape into the meeting?' 'Oh,' I said, 'I just like to hear my voice.' Kent is really against the wall because he doesn't quite know where he fits in the advertising business. 'You probably can't hear my voice on that recorder,' he says. I said, 'Come on, Kent, come on, I know it was you speaking.' He couldn't even take it as a joke. 'Oh, no,' Kent said, 'I know my own voice. I know when I talk and I can tell if I have my voice on a tape recorder.'

I passed by another office, a guy named Marks, and he vaulted over a little marble coffee table he had in his office and flew into the hall. 'Why'd you do it, Jerry?' Marks asked. 'To hear my voice,' I said, and I was getting a bit tired of saying it, too. 'It's a very bad business,' he said, and turned away. Finally I got to the Creative Director of the World and there were the rest of the creative review board.

'It turned me off,' said one guy. 'Why did you do it?' asked another. The Creative Director of the World said, 'Will you hand it over, please?' They really were quite disturbed. As I walked out of the office I couldn't resist saying, 'Gee, I think this should be a practice in all of your creative review sessions. You know, I think it would be fantastic if you installed a videotape set so that you could tape these things and have them running for the rest of the people in the agency. It would be very helpful.' One guy, a good friend of mine, said, 'It will be a long time before we tape any other review session and it will be an even longer time before you come back to the creative review board.'

Well, what's the story here? Fear. Basically, these guys have never, never been on record before. The noncreative people who work in the creative department are so used to lying to themselves that they can write – these guys were afraid of the tape recorder. It represented truth. These guys had been kidding each other all their lives, and like this tape recorder meant something. The tape recorder could put them away. The tape recorder was truth; they couldn't deny truth and they couldn't live with it. They could carry on, but they couldn't face that little thirty-dollar tape recorder. Some of these people are so adept at kidding themselves and everybody else that they're professionals at it.

They never held another creative review board meeting at Bates – at least not while I was there. That session with me ended it. And the word got out in the agency, 'Did you really do it?' And I said, 'Of course I did.' The story picked up the entire creative department. Everybody in the creative department felt – Wow! – we've got something going here. It was like a victory for a lot of guys who had been getting killed by the noncreative creative experts.

Sometimes the pressure on the creative people isn't as obvious as a review board. It can get subtle, very subtle. A one-on-one kind of thing. I worked at an agency where there was a guy whom I referred to as the Mount Everest of Fear. He worked for the vice-president, the man named David whom we called The Klutz, and to this day I've never met a more fearful guy. I was really just a punk kid then, I couldn't have been more than twenty-five, and David used this man the way the Green Hornet used to use his trusty valet Cato. I would walk into David's office to show him an ad, and David would always drive me insane because he would always come out and say, 'I don't like it.' He never said, 'I don't like it because . . .' Just 'I don't like it.' And I'd say, 'Come on, David, you must have a reason for not liking it. There's got to be something there that you can put your finger on.' Good old David would shake his head and say, 'Jerry, this just doesn't make it.' Then he'd say, 'All right, I'm going to prove it. I'll call in Cato and let's see if Cato likes it.'

He trusted Cato. Cato would come into the office and stand around, just like a buzzard, hovering over the ad. David always had a secret way of looking at Cato to tell Cato whether he really liked or hated the ad. David would say, 'Cato, what do you think of this ad?' I never could get the key word but Cato always could read David. Cato would look at David and read his face and say, 'You're right, David, it doesn't make it.' Or David would call him in and say, 'Cato, what about this one?' Quick as a flash Cato would pick up the sign and say, 'Hey, David, that's a great ad.' Then David would turn to me and say, 'You see, Jerry, I told you, it's a great ad.'

One day I showed David an ad and he hated it, so he called in Cato, but evidently forgot to flash the signal. Maybe David would twitch his eyes, but this time he must have forgotten. David asked Cato what he thought and zap, Cato blew the signal. David was standing there and Cato's trying to pick up the signal. But no signal. 'Well, David,' Cato started to say, and then he stopped. Meanwhile, David was getting impatient and kept saying, 'What about this one, Cato?' Cato is fumbling. 'Let me read the headline again,' he said. He's reading the headline, and he's looking at David trying to get some kind of playback and David's standing there and no playback is showing up. The guy's whole life was going before him. I'd never seen anything like it in my life.

I couldn't stand watching this guy die any longer, so I finally said, 'Cato, listen, David hates this ad. Thinks it stinks.' It was like rescuing a drowning person. Then Cato went into his act. 'Of course,' he said. 'Now the problem with this ad is the layout and . . .' All he needed was to know how David stood on the ad and then he was able to fly.

I really don't think creative people are afraid of losing their jobs at the whim of the agency, but there is one thing that drives them up the wall: fear of losing their talent, their abilities. Everybody I know feels this pressure. Is this ability something like magic? Will it ever just disappear? Will the day come when you sit down and suddenly you don't feel the same thing working in you the way you used to? You can't write any more. The words don't go together.

One of the ways Charlie Goldschmidt of Daniel & Charles had of spurring his troops on was to play on this fear that copywriters have: he used to plague me with it and everybody else, too. 'Well, kid,' he would say, 'what do you think? You haven't had an idea in about three weeks. You're starting to fake it, aren't you? You're trying to coast because it happens sometimes, you've got it one day and the next day it's gone.' And he would do this, he would pressure his people this way in the hope of shaking them up and getting them out of the doldrums.

Listen, somebody is paying you thirty-five, forty grand a year to do this thing, copywriting, or being an art director, and you're bound to have this fear of going dry. A fantastic art director named Bob Gage at Doyle, Dane once made a speech on fear, what it was, how to combat it. He described it as the fear of going dry and then he discovered that you can never go dry, that there is no mystique, there's no magic to it, you can't turn off like that. Gage said that when he found himself going dry, it was a matter of being faced with a problem that had to be solved and that he could always solve the problem the same old way he had solved it years before. He said that going dry was simply becoming impatient with problem-solving in the same old way.

Most writers and art directors become impatient when they've got a tough problem, and that's where they get into trouble. They play, they dance, they do everything in their power to look as though they're producing advertising. And the minute they come in your office you know they're pretending. They're cold and they're dry and they know it and you know it and they know you know it.

I've seen guys who couldn't produce an ad for six or eight months, they'd be so tied up in knots. During that time, these guys would have to dance. Charlie Goldschmidt was a guy who started out as a copywriter and became a brilliant agency president. He's a fantastic guy who could walk into a room, shake your hand, and tell you what your hang-ups were as he was shaking your hand. He always amazed me that way. He always knew everyone's weak points, their panic buttons, and he knew just how to push them to get you started.

When I was working for Charlie I went through a bad dry spell where I did zip for three or four months. Nothing. I would sit in the room and nothing would happen. And you know when you're coming up with ads and you know when you're not. I would fake it. I would come up with mediocre solutions to problems. And you start to think about it, and it starts to bug you and you don't know quite what to do. So to get by you start to dance a little bit.

But Charlie caught it. He knew it. And he would walk into your room and say, 'Did you ever stop to think that that's it? You might have just dried up? You haven't got another idea in you. Well, kid, stay loose.'

Those were always his exact words. First a slap on the back and then, 'Well, kid, stay loose.' You didn't stay exactly loose after he left you, but sooner or later – usually sooner – you shaped up.

Another problem with copywriters and art directors is the problem of recognition. There are a lot of copywriters who get mixed up and think they're Faulkner or Hemingway. They sit there and they work and they mold and they play and when it's over they've written something that's absolutely beautiful but they forget one thing. It's within the confines of a page that's bought by a media director. What kills most copywriters is that people don't buy *Life* magazine to read their ads. People don't buy *Gourmet* to read their ad for Bombay Gin. People are buying *Gourmet* to read the recipes, and the ads are just an intrusion on people's time. That is why it is our job to get more attention than anything else. Nobody buys any magazine to read an ad. But a lot of guys act as though this is what is happening. This guy sat there, he's written this thing, and as far as he's concerned, this is it. Then he meets someone at a party and is explaining with a great deal of pride that he is a copywriter and the person says, 'Oh, you put the captions on the bottom of the pictures.'

I've had account executives who sit down and practically cry, asking me to change something because the client's going to yell. 'We're going to lose the account.' That's the big word all the time from the account executives to the copywriters and the art directors.

Once a year the New York copywriters hold a party. Last year it was held in a photographer's studio with maybe five hundred people jammed into a room that can really only hold about two hundred. With a rock-and-roll band that's blasting so you can't hear yourself think. Copywriters aren't the kind of people who usually go to parties. But this is the party they all go to, this is where they're going to get that job or they're going to meet that guy or they're going to do something that is going to change their lives.

They try to make their contacts. Any creative director who walked from one end of the room to the other had at least eight people tell him, 'Can I bring my portfolio up and see you on Monday?' One after another. 'Hi, how are you? I hear things are going very good. Can I bring my book up to see you on Monday? The place I'm at is really terrible; can't stand it, I can't stay there another day.'

Then I met a guy at the party, and I knew him fairly well. He's a very good writer and kind of a strange kid, very quiet, but nothing unusual about him. He was making about thirty thousand a year. At that party he was very uptight.

What was it all about? He'd been fired that morning. And he said, 'I've got five hundred dollars in the bank, I make thirty thousand a year, and I pay two hundred and eighty-four dollars a month in rent.' Who knows where his money went? Clothes, apartment, chicks, I don't know. But he'd blown all his money and there he was, thirty-one or thirty-two, and I tell you he was a desperate kid, he really was. I had never seen him like that. 'What am I going to do?' he asked. 'How about some free-lance?' I said. He shook his head. He must have made twenty calls that day because every time I said, 'Did you call Ned, did you call Ron, did you call Ed?' he'd shake his head yes. He'd called everybody worth calling. So he's run out of names to call and he's only one day out of a job. Now he starts with the headhunters and asks them to start setting up appointments for him.

He's a good writer. That's the scary part of it. He blew his last job essentially because he's a very tough sport. He won't take any garbage. He had been working for Leber, Katz & Paccione, and Patch finally couldn't take any more lip from him. So out he went.

Before Paccione he had worked for Daniel & Charles and got fired because he couldn't get along with Larry Dunst, who then was the creative director and now is the president. The job after Daniel & Charles fell apart the same way.

On about the fourth job out, he's not going to be so quick to be such a smart-ass. He mentioned to me that he had called a small agency which is really not an advertising agency but rather a dress house; they do all of that *Seventh Avenue* advertising you see in *Women's Wear Daily* and the Sunday *Times* magazine section. Very big on girdle and bra ads. Anyhow, the owner of the agency told him to come on by on Monday, that is, the guy said, 'I'll see you Monday if you want to come in and say hello.' Now this agency is one of the all-time bad places – it may be the worst agency in America. And he's thinking seriously of going there for a lot of bread – if they'll have him. So he's scared, he's got a bad weekend ahead of him, and when I left him he was quaking he was so scared.

Paccione already had replaced this guy. He found a twenty-two-year-old who thought advertising was the living end and hired her for eight grand a year. I had talked to her a couple of times about coming to work for us. No sooner do I finish talking to the guy who's out of work when I run into this kid. 'Hi,' she says, full of life, 'I got my job. I'm working. I'm starting with Leber, Katz, Paccione on Monday.' 'That's terrific,' I said, and I started to figure it out. Patch hired this kid for eight grand, and he's saving twenty-two grand a year already by getting rid of the thirty-grand guy. Plus he's gotten rid of somebody who was a pain in the ass to him. And this young chick now is on her way to making a lot of money. Her next job she'll be able to grab off ten grand, the one after that fifteen grand, then twenty-one and then up to thirty a year. And then she'll find herself in the same position as the guy who just got fired. And she'll start to get a little nervous because there will be somebody else hot coming up.

It's really not unlike baseball. You don't have that many good years to perform in. You've got about seven, eight, or maybe nine years when you're hot and everything you do works and they're calling you for a job and the headhunters are crying for you, and then there's that long downhill slide. Which is why the shrinks are making out so well. And everybody knows that day is going to come to them. It used to kill me that I never saw a copywriter over forty. Very, very few. There are one or two guys worth mentioning but that's it. I can't figure out where they go after forty. But they leave. There must be an island somewhere that is populated only by elephants, copywriters and art directors. I can see it now. One tiny island jammed with old elephants, burned-out copywriters and art directors. That must be where they go.

I wonder what happened to most of the guys I started out in business with. I began in the mailroom of Ruthrauff & Ryan, and the only guy that I know of still in advertising from those days is Evan Stark, who is now at Doyle, Dane. Forget about where the guys are. Where are the agencies? Ruthrauff & Ryan is gone. I once went looking for a job at the Biow Agency. Gone. Donahue & Coe. Gone. Cecil & Presby. You ever hear of that one? Lennen & Newell used to be Lennen & Mitchell. You'd better amend that thought about the island with the elephants and the ex-copywriters: they also got on that island one hell of a lot of dead agencies.

Fashions change. So does advertising. The physical look of advertising changes from year to year. Last year's ads don't look as good as this year's. I get tired of looking at my old ads. They bore me. The kids are changing everything – language, clothes, style, and the visual arts.

The schools are breeding kids like nobody's business. Don't you think that when Patch got rid of that thirty-two-year-old guy that a lot of guys felt a cold draft down their necks? Of course they did. I know a $40,000-a-year art director working for Patch who's thinking about that eight-grand-a-year copywriter and he's saying to himself, 'What if Patch goes out and finds an eight-grand-a-year art director – where do I go with my forty grand a year?' Phones are ringing all over town. Everybody's changing jobs. It's like musical chairs – you can't keep up. The kids are death on forty-grand-a-year art directors and copywriters. Pure death.

Maybe we're in the middle of a recession and we don't know it. Advertising people can usually predict a recession a lot sooner than the rest of the country. I know when the economy is going to get a little rotten and I can smell it because the advertisers slowly start to pull back. Agency presidents start to get a little more nervous than usual, and the whole pullback works its way down to the copywriters who won't get hired.

At that annual copywriter's party I went to last year, there was a lot of fear and the whole room was kind of nervous. What is happening is simply that there aren't enough jobs to go around. There have been periods in this business when the phones were always ringing and you couldn't keep up with all of the openings. Not today – and I wonder if it is going to get even worse. It's interesting that in that room of five hundred people – mostly copywriters – there were only four or five people I would hire. Forget about the party; in the entire city there are maybe twenty-five copywriters worth mentioning. The whole city. You're talking about an agency like J. Walter Thompson which had only one writer whose work I admire – Ron Rosenfeld – and he just quit there after one year. Forget it after that. An agency like Compton must have fifty or sixty copywriters. The only guy whose stuff I can look at is my ex-partner's – Ned Tolmach. Four years ago I went to that party and this year it was an entirely different group of people. I found about ten or fifteen standbys who always show up, and the rest, you know, it's tall, gangly kids with pimples and girls who have decided it's the most glamorous business in the world and they're really out to make it.

The same sort of fear that copywriters show in public – like at the party – bugs them in private. For example, if a writer's campaign is killed, forget it, the guy is lost for a couple of months. And these campaigns are like babies. These guys sit there and they love their campaigns and they look at their ads and they take them out and mount them. You're talking about a piece of paper, and the copywriter puts it on a piece of mounting board and wraps it in Cellophane and he carries it around to show people.

The dilemma is that the good writers in this town are those who are really not afraid. You've got to be loose. It's the one business where you've got to be so loose when you're sitting down to work that you can't sit there and worry about what's going on next door or am I going to lose my job. And there are very few people like that in the creative end of advertising. Practically none. Most copywriters have the same background: middle class to lower middle class. All the copywriters in town have read *Portnoy's Complaint* and they all say, 'That's my life. I was Portnoy except that I would never do such a thing to a piece of liver.'

Everybody in advertising in mixed up – but especially the creative people. Your whole life is screwed up. You're not the same kind of guy once you get into the business. It's hard to describe a business that really gets into your blood the way advertising does. After you've worked in it for a while, you're not the same person that you ordinarily would be. I often wonder how I would have been or how I would behave if I had gone into the aluminum-siding business.

What happens to some guys is – well, I'll draw the analogy to sports again. Baseball has its hot players and the next year the hot players cool off, and what happens is that their salaries drop and they get optioned out to Toledo.

There was a really good creative director in New York a few years ago who either lost it, blew it, or God knows. Anyhow, the next thing you hear he's out in Chicago working for an agency. When you go to Chicago that's like being optioned to Newark if you're playing for the Yankees when the Yankees were the only thing going in baseball. I don't know where you go after Chicago. He's making a lot of money but it doesn't mean anything. It's still Chicago, the minors. Some guys go to Pittsburgh, the minors. You go to Cleveland, you're still in the minors. When you talk about the major leagues you're talking about New York, with Los Angeles coming up fast. In between New York and L.A. you have very little except for Leo Burnett in Chicago.

It's very strange out of town, especially when a guy from New York is invited by some locals someplace to make a speech. There's real hero worship. They all want to grow up and come to New York, and when you show up in their town they expect you to turn the water cooler into a wine cooler. They look at you and they say, 'Jesus, he's here. He's going to tell us how to do it.' And then you find they know everything about you.

I was down in Charlotte, North Carolina, one time to make a speech and I sat next to a guy who said, 'Remember when you did that ad for Esquire Sox?' I didn't even remember ever working on Esquire Sox, much less the ad the guy was talking about, but this guy wouldn't let up: 'Don't you remember the ad? There's a man in the ad who is talking and the girl is standing in the background . . .' And then the ad came back to me. But this guy had like literally collected these things and was following me, and it's crazy but I'm a scrapbook someplace in Charlotte, North Carolina.

A friend of mine once went out to Cleveland to make a speech and when he came back he called me and said, 'There's a guy in Cleveland who knows more about you than your wife.' He mentioned the guy's name and of course I'd never heard of him, and my friend says the guy from Cleveland has a scrapbook on me with every ad I ever wrote, every speech I ever made, and every advertising column I ever wrote for *Marketing/Communications*. This is the out-of-town story.

The standard word around Madison Avenue is that the out-of-towners love to be put down. If you want to make a speech out of town you've got to tell them that they're no good. If you ever tell them that they're good, they'll hate you for it. They really sit there waiting for you to come in and say, 'Boy, are you guys bad. I mean, are you *bad*. You know, in New York none of you would ever get a job.' And they sit there and say, 'Yeah, that's New York advertising talking.' It's crazy.

In Los Angeles, the guy they've promoted to sainthood is Gene Case. Case is a beautiful, beautiful writer who recently formed his own agency with another beauty, Helmut Crone, an art director. Case had worked at Jack Tinker & Partners and Crone was from Doyle, Dane.

Case is invited out to the Coast to make a speech, and they pick him up at the airport. They're driving away from the airport on their way to get a drink or something and Case is looking out of the window as they drive in. If you've ever driven in on Sepulveda Boulevard, you know it is not much to look at. Anyhow, Case makes the speech and immediately he says, 'I've got to get out of here. I've got to fly out of this town, I hate it.' The L.A. guys are looking at Case as if he's crazy. They want to take him out to dinner. But he's insisting that they take him back to the airport, he's had his look at L.A., and he's had enough. He says to them, 'I know this place. I used to present to the Carnation Milk account out here when I worked for Jack Tinker, and they were always nasty to me. I can't stand this town. You've got to take me to the airport.' So they shake their heads, bundle Case back on a plane to New

York and today. he's a legend out there. 'Gene Case, wasn't he fantastic?' they say. Case, of course, produced the ultimate putdown.

It's nice – out of town. A different kind of advertising. It's a slower and much easier life because, let's face it, where could you be banished to if you're working in Cleveland? I mean, where could they send you? Akron? In New York, you could always wind up in Cleveland, but like in Cleveland there's nothing worse. So the people don't have the same fears. They don't have the same salaries, either. They don't have the same relationships with clients. It's not advertising the way I know it. In New York you have real stars – copy guys, art directors, creative people, television directors – who are good and they know it. Some of these creative people command higher salaries than the president of an agency in Cleveland might get. There is an emphasis on the creative guy in New York. Agencies put up with the craziness to get the creative. There's no creativity in Cleveland, very little originality.

It's a whole different game. It's maybe advertising the way it used to be in 1942. The president of the agency still gets out on the golf course and plays with his client, the president of Acme Steel. The president of the agency lives very well and the rest of the people in the agency are just working people. They don't make big salaries. There are no glamour people in, say, Cleveland. There's nobody sitting in Cleveland saying, 'I want to be like somebody else in Cleveland.' They live vicariously and get their glamour from New York.

Cleveland will eventually change. The creative revolution will eventually get there. In New York, advertising is changing drastically and rapidly. Creative people are getting more clout. It is a provable fact that the so-called creative agencies are the ones that are growing the fastest. But I also have the feeling that life for the creative side of an agency will always be tough. Now you've got creative review boards made up of red noses and blue veins. Who knows? In twenty years perhaps pot will be legalized. It depresses me to think that in twenty years there still will be creative review boards, except that the board will not be made up of red noses. Instead, you'll have a bunch of old guys with very funny pupils looking at your work. A bunch of dilated pupils checking you out. *That* kind of nonsense will never change.

CHAPTER SEVEN
THE JOLLY GREEN GIANT AND OTHER STORIES

'There is a great deal of advertising that is much better than the product. When that happens, all that the good advertising will do is put you out of business faster ... All the great advertising in the world can never straighten out the stewardess who wakes up cranky one morning. There is nothing in the world an agency can do about the gas station attendant in One Horse Stand, Nebraska, who has a hangover ...'

I don't want to give the impression that the new creative agencies can do no wrong. They can do plenty of wrong, and in fact they can do so much wrong they can blow the whole thing. Creative or not.

Several years ago two guys got together to form a new agency. They planned the agency along the lines of William Esty. Now William Esty is a very successful agency. It must bill somewhere in the neighborhood of $140 million a year, which is good billing. And William Esty has a very shrewd concept: Don't take on a lot of accounts, just a few high-ticket, very large accounts. I think Esty has Sun Oil, Colgate, National Biscuit, American Home Products, Hunt-Wesson and only a few others. They can't have more than ten or fifteen accounts, but all of them bill very high. Esty supposedly has the fewest number of employees for the number of accounts of any agency in town. You're supposed to have something like eight employees for every $1 million in billing. Esty handles their accounts with maybe six employees for every $1 million. It is a very efficiently run agency, beautifully handled, and they can't lose. They make nothing but money at Esty. They don't care for too much publicity at Esty; all they want to do is their job – and count the dollars.

They hold onto their accounts because with that small a number you really pay a lot of attention to them. Figure it out: the president has maybe ten or eleven guys to worry about each day – the chairman of the boards of the various accounts. He can make ten or eleven calls a day to see how his accounts are, he can have lunch with each chairman of the board in the space of two weeks. Esty pays a lot of attention to their accounts and they make sure their accounts are happy. And, believe me, they are.

Anyhow, let's get back to the two guys who formed that

other agency a few years ago, and let's call them Manny and Moe. The first year Manny and Moe began they had zero billing and then they got hot. At the end of the first year they had $6 million in billing, and they added a little bit to that the second year. During the third year they really got hot – they got so hot their billing went up to like $20 million. The fourth year they must have hit $40 million. Well, they hit their high of $40 million, and then they died, absolutely died. They managed to lose more business than I'll ever see in my lifetime. It got so you couldn't pick up Phil Dougherty's column in *The Times* without reading of another client leaving Manny and Moe.

When Manny and Moe set up their agency along the lines of Esty, they said to themselves, 'We'll load ourselves up with some high-ticket accounts and we'll coin money.' They forgot one thing. These people come – and go, too. It is very hard to keep a long-lasting relationship with an account when you are bored with it. And they blew it all because they got bored. Manny decided he was going to save the world, which is O.K. if your business is good. Moe decided *he* was going to beat the horses, which is even tougher than saving the world.

Manny got very interested in gun control and political campaigns. That was good. But you've got to be careful. There are guys running around Madison Avenue who also have guns and they are always trying to knock you off. You might be an account sitting out in the waiting room with a hell of a problem, and you're looking for Manny. When you gave them the account, they promised you Manny would be working on it. Where's Manny? Well, right now Manny is out in Jackson Hole, Wyoming, working on a political campaign for a guy who's running for sewer commissioner of Jackson Hole. Manny thinks this guy has a future in politics, and he's trying to make him into something much bigger than the sewer commissioner. Terrific, except if you're a client and you want to see Manny you've got to figure out how to get to Wyoming.

Where's Moe? Well, Moe is studying the racing form, and when Moe starts handicapping the fifth at Belmont it can get a little confusing. Moe may have been the only agency president in America who would show up at meetings with binoculars around his neck. He became so track-oriented that he didn't know what was going on at his own agency. A media guy would come in to Moe and ask him, 'Where are we going to spend this million dollars from the client?' Moe would say, 'How many furlongs?'

And there was no management. They hired a guy to be president but he was nothing but a caretaker. Manny was out saving the world through advertising, and Moe was out at the track every day losing his shirt. Clients were being left out in the halls waiting to see somebody. They used to wait hours. Creative people used to take them into their offices and give them coffee while they were waiting. Clients are human and finally they got to the point where they started telling Manny and Moe, 'Screw you. I mean your advertising isn't even good any more, and who needs all the abuse?' The agency folded a couple of years ago.

All of the newer agencies blow something now and then. Even the guys at Doyle, Dane. A couple of years ago they did a campaign for a new beer out by the Rheingold Brewery people – the new stuff was called Gablinger's Beer. The thing about Gablinger's was that it was very low in calories, and the thought was, 'We'll sell this to all those guys who drink beer and want to lose weight.'

Somewhere, somehow, they blew it. Somebody in research made the first mistake, which was thinking that beer drinkers wanted to lose weight while drinking beer. Not true. Twenty percent of the people in this country who buy beer drink about 80 percent of all the beer consumed. I have an image in my mind of your typical beer drinker: the man never has a shirt on. He's always in his undershirt, one of those old-fashioned undershirts, not a tee shirt. I may be wrong there, but I could swear that your typical beer drinker is proud of his beer belly. There he is, swilling beer all day long, and the only thing he has to show for it is his belly. It's his sign of masculinity.

Now, you have a great example of one error compounding another error compounding still another error. So the first error – thinking that these guys want to lose weight – leads to the second error, which is that you can build a campaign on this attitude and spend $5 million and tie up the whole beer market because all of these beer people want to lose weight. Campaigns will work only if the initial premise is true. But it's like the Leaning Tower of Pisa: the first brick was crooked and after that everything started going sideways, and you wind up with a fucking silly-looking building or you wind up with a pretty terrible campaign. Since the first premise in Gablinger's case was wrong, the thing went bad all up and down the line. Beer drinkers want to be fat. They love to watch their bellies. Figure it out: they like looking at their bellies because they never see their feet. Go into the bars right now. These guys start drinking at nine o'clock in the morning – and they have their more than one by 9:05 a.m. And they drink and they drink and drink and drink, and this is the beer market.

The only thing you have to worry about in selling beer is to give these guys enough time to waste. I mean, don't give these guys anything to do in which they have to use their hands, other than bowling. Bowling is O.K. because all they have to do is get up every seven minutes or so and roll a ball and then sit down as fast as they can and start drinking beer again.

Beer companies shouldn't sponsor golf matches because golf is death on a beer drinker. If you're out on the fourteenth hole, you can't have a beer unless you throw away the clubs and lug beer around instead. Just find enough leisure time for the beer drinkers, that's your only worry. Leisure time, in a beer drinker's mind, means all they have to do is reach for a glass or for a bottle. Maybe they'll have to get up from the television set and go to the refrigerator, but that's it. Your real beer drinker can sit home watching television and polish off two six-packs a night. If he's thirsty, or it's hot out, make that even more. His wife will drink only four or five cans because she's suddenly decided that she really shouldn't drink more than a six-pack a night – it won't look good. So you've got like three six-packs a family a night. And you can count their kid in if he's over ten years old.

Look at these people at the supermarket. They're pushing market baskets piled high with beer, a couple of packages of hot dogs, and that's it. Eighteen cans of beer a night except on Friday, which is party night when they switch to a clean undershirt. And on Friday you've got to figure that the guy is going to double his weekday consumption.

I went to a Yankee game one night last year and there was a real beer drinker in front of me, the genuine thing. I was watching him, and he made the night for the kid selling beer. He stopped once for peanuts, but that was a mistake because he didn't finish them. He knocked the beer off just like pills – I swear he must have drunk ten or twelve cans during that nine-inning game. He didn't get up for the seventh-inning stretch, which doesn't indicate that he wasn't a Yankee fan. It was simply a matter that his legs weren't moving too good at the time. There he was, sitting and drinking, and when the game was over he showed that he was a true fan. I got up to leave and he was still sitting there. Sitting there and looking out at the field, but he was staring straight ahead. A real beer drinker, with a real beer belly. Now you know if I had come up to him after the game and said, 'Hey, buddy, do you know you just knocked off three thousand calories in all that beer? Why don't you switch to something that won't make you fat?' – do you know what he would have done? He would have punched me in the mouth – that is, if he could have gotten his hands free.

Now it is theoretically possible to sell Gablinger's Beer. It's a good idea, but not for Bohack, or A & P, or Piggly Wiggly. You sell it to Gristede's because it's a carriage-trade product. The lady who shops in Gristede's might pick up one six-pack because she likes the notion that it's low on calories.

The beer business is very strange. Go into Costello's, which is an old-time bar on Third Avenue in New York – go into there any night and pick the guy who has just staggered out of the men's room and is trying to climb back on his bar stool. Go up to this cat and ask him what he thinks of Rheingold Beer. He doesn't know zip about Rheingold Beer but he'll focus his eyes and swear to you that Maureen Harrington got cheated out of winning the Miss Rheingold contest back in 1961 because a lot of votes for the girl named Beverly came in from Brooklyn on the last day of the contest. You think I'm kidding? There are guys in New York who went into mourning the day they discontinued the contest in 1965.

Interesting thing about the contest. One of the marketing geniuses behind the campaign was supposedly trying to make it with almost every Miss Rheingold who came down the pike. That is one hell of a lot of Miss Rheingolds. But practically every one of them. And this marketing genius one day woke up and couldn't feel his legs. So he went to Europe to dry out. I mean, he's probably thirty-three or thirty-four now, but he can't walk. He's sitting there in his wheelchair with a little gray shawl over his legs and one hell of a lot of memories. He got tired of the contest. Bored. It can happen; he's entitled. So Rheingold went to Doyle, Dane and they produced those ethnic commercials – Doyle, Dane, let's face it, does not have a stunning beer record in New York City.

The ethnic commercials were beautifully done. Not only did they not sell beer; they antagonized a lot of people. Let's say our beer drinker is an Italian. They had an Italian commercial with a lot of people running around and dancing and saying '*Mamma mia*' and things like that, and during the commercial the Italian beer drinker was very happy. He had a nice warm feeling for Rheingold. Then, one day he's watching television and a group of Poles show up dancing a polka and carrying on a lot. This drives the Italian up the wall. He says, 'I won't touch the same beer those lousy Poles are drinking.' They had a Jewish commercial, they had Germans, they had the Irish, they even had a Negro blues singer surrounded by a bunch of guys who today would be identified as Black Panthers. They had everybody but the WASPs, and everybody knows WASPs don't know from beer. Instead of getting everybody together in the spirit of good fellowship and all that jazz, they blew the campaign because all of the groups really hated each other.

Beer advertising can be very tricky. Young & Rubicam turned out some terrific ads on Bert and Harry Piel, the Piel Brothers. Everybody liked Bert and Harry, all the intellectuals loved them. Good old Bert and Harry: they laughed at the product, they had fun. The big mistake with that campaign was that it got people to taste Piel's Beer. A guy would take one sip of it and say, 'Screw Bert and Harry, like they were a lot of fun and I like to look at them on the late news but they're not going to make me drink this stuff.' It's a case of 'You can lead a horse to water but you can't make him drink,' especially if he's tried the stream once and it tastes terrible. And that was it. Bert and Harry never came back.

As far as I'm concerned, the best beer advertising today is Schaefer's. It really gets to the beer drinkers; it has a very simple, very meaningful message for the real drinkers. 'The one beer to have when you're having more than one.' Boy, does that message come across to those guys. They really understand it. Wow! And the guy grabs another can of beer. What a red flag that line is! Here I am, having more than one. As a matter of fact, I'm having seventeen at one sitting, and my eyes are getting glassy. And Schaefer is the only beer that will make me feel great when this binge is all over.

Schaefer is done by Batten, Barton, Durstine & Osborne. They're an agency that hasn't distinguished itself for much other than Schaefer, Pepsi-Cola, Dodge, and Chiquita Banana. (But they were brilliant with Chiquita Banana. They sold bananas without laughing. They gave the banana an identity and, you know, they literally made banana history. I mean, you never see any other banana commercials, do you?) It's an interesting thing when a good campaign comes out – there usually are a hundred guys who take credit for it. I know of at least nine guys who modestly say they came up with the line about the one beer to have when you're having more than one. A number of friends of mine at B.B.D.O. tell me that a guy named Jim Jordan, who is a creative director, is the guy who did the campaign.

Compare the Schaefer campaign with the Ballantine Beer campaign created by Stan Freberg – the campaign using the takeoff on *Portnoy's Complaint*, except they call it 'Ballantine's Complaint.' Very cute stuff but it falls into that trap of having the wrong initial premise: How many beer drinkers have read *Portnoy's Complaint*? Forget the book. How many beer drinkers can read? One of the commercials shows a guy named Ballantine lying on a shrink's couch complaining about how he left the brewery in the hands of his family while he went on a trip and the family loused up the beer. How many beer drinkers give a goddamn if Ballantine had a problem with his family? How many beer drinkers have ever been to a shrink? How many of them ever heard of Philip Roth? As far as they're concerned, that beer is off the books. They might have had a can of Ballantine at a ball game once, and that's it. They won't drink Ballantine for anybody any more. These guys know where they're understood and loved – and I mean *loved*: Schaefer.

Rheingold nowadays is doing things with ten-minute heads. Nonsense. There isn't a beer drinker alive who will sit and watch the head on his beer disappear in ten minutes, timed, by the way, with a stopwatch. Your beer drinker figures he can put two and a half beers away in ten minutes, forget about your head.

Pabst Blue Ribbon does nice commercials with a nostalgic twist – usually a bunch of people in straw hats at a picnic. But I'm convinced that the only kind of nostalgia that will sell beer is a guy standing in a bar saying, 'Hey, let's have a beer for good old Joe DiMaggio. And hey, what about Dixie Walker? And now let's have one for Carl Furillo.' Nostalgia is not a bunch of guys clowning around at an old-timey picnic. Nostalgia is Joe D. picking one off in center field. That's what nostalgia is all about for the beer drinker.

The last figures I looked at for beer sales showed Schaefer climbing out of sight. Budweiser is still the biggest-selling beer in the country. But their sales aren't climbing the way Schaefer's are. They've tried a number of campaigns and a bunch of commercials. So they've got their horses *schlepping*, and that's O.K. if you like horses, which I don't happen to. The best commercial of theirs I've seen lately has Ed McMahon, who is a great guy to sell beer, standing there and saying, 'Folks, it's that time you've all been waiting for. It's time to pick up two packs of Bud.' There is no particular reason why a guy should pick up *two* instead of one, but it gives a lot of beer drinkers inspiration. And these drinkers are usually pretty short of inspiration. So they say to themselves, 'Gee, you're right, Ed, I should have picked up two instead of one.' So people are buying double. You don't save any money. They just tell you this is the time of year you've got to buy two of them rather than one.

Bud does very well – and Schaefer – but that's about it. Not long ago Jack Tinker did a campaign for Carling's Black Label, which said that we have our breweries close to every city so our beer is always fresh. They were trying to sell quality to these guys. Fresh as opposed to stale. Beer drinkers know the difference in quality. They know what stale beer is: it's what they taste in their mouth the next morning when they wake up. They know that taste well, but they wouldn't buy Carling's because it's fresh. So the campaign bombed out.

Although Doyle, Dane is so-so with beer, they're absolutely great on hard booze. I don't know why. Maybe it's because most of the guys working at Doyle, Dane drink only hard booze and couldn't care less about beer. They took a perfectly ordinary scotch, Chivas Regal, and upgraded it, gave it snob appeal. They convinced people to trade up in booze so that when somebody spent $7.50 for a fifth of Chivas Regal he was convinced that the booze was worth it. The ads they did for

Chivas were beautifully designed – elegant. Another great booze campaign of theirs, which was done by Ron Rosenfeld, was the Calvert's 'soft whiskey' line. To this day I don't know what the hell 'soft whiskey' means, but it evidently meant something to the guys who were pouring rotgut down their throats, because 'soft whiskey' sold like hell.

The worst idea for a booze campaign that I can remember was the one put out several years ago by Schenley's. A marketing executive at Schenley insisted that their agency have a mascot, and the mascot was named Sunny the Rooster. Sunny the Rooster was supposed to equal that sunny morning flavor. The marketing executive was convinced that if he could tell people that they wouldn't be hung over and feel like dogs the next day he could sell a lot of booze. What they were trying to say – and couldn't – was, 'Listen, buddy, if you drink our booze you'll never wake up having to look in your wallet to find out who you are and all that kind of nonsense. You drink our stuff and you'll be perfectly all right.'

What they did was to hang about seven agencies with Sunny the Rooster. So there you have seven agencies trying to come up with a campaign built around that sunny morning flavor and feeling. They turned out Sunny the Roosters galore. Thank God, the campaign never ran. Nobody came up with anything that was halfway decent. Nobody knew whether the agencies they tried were bad or whether Sunny the Rooster was just another crazy notion who should have had his head chopped off early in the game. A lot of guys spent a lot of money on Sunny.

Sometimes great campaigns work, bring in the customers, but then there are other things happening that kill you. Ed McCabe, who now has his own agency of Scali, McCabe, Sloves, used to work at Carl Ally. Ed McCabe is maybe one of the five top writers in town. He did the Horn & Hardart campaign when he was at Ally, and it was great. It was so great that it reached all kinds of people – including a girl I'll call Betty-Sue. Now Betty-Sue comes to New York from Kneejerk, North Carolina, and she goes to work for Delehanty, Kurnit & Geller when I was working there. Betty-Sue is a terrific kid except she had a little problem with the English language – she couldn't speak it. That is, she spoke but you couldn't understand her. One Monday morning she comes up to me and she says, 'Jer, I bin reading those Horn and Hardart ads, the ones which say "It May Not Be Fancy but It's Good." I said, 'What'd you say, Betty-Sue?' She said, 'Bin reading the Horn and Hardart ads, "It May Not Be." 'Oh,' I said, 'you've been reading the Horn and Hardart ads?'

She said, 'And I decided to go to Horn and Hardart, and I had some of their beans and the beans were goooooood, and I had some lemonmrang pah and it was goooooood, and then I had some coffee and it was goooooood. And then the man sitting across the way exposed himself.'

Unfortunately, this was one of the problems that Ed McCabe faced. He could come up with the selling line that reached a Betty-Sue, but he couldn't go around and take care of the occasional guy who was walking into Horn & Hardart wearing a raincoat and making quick flashes. But the guy wrote a classic line that sold and got a lot of people to come to Horn & Hardart.

There is a great deal of advertising that is much better than the product. When that happens, all that the good advertising will do is put you out of business faster. There have been some cases where the product had to come up to the advertising but when the product fails to do that, the advertiser will eventually run into a lot of trouble.

Let's take the airlines again. They have great advertising and the problem is, planes get stacked up, the air-traffic controllers are either walking out on strike or threatening to walk out, you can sit on the ground at La Guardia Airport for two hours trying to get out of town, and what sometimes happens to baggage shouldn't happen to a dog. The airlines that don't have service which lives up to the advertising have trouble. The greatest living commercial of all time for Mohawk Airlines will not get me on a Mohawk plane. Let me change to an airline that's a lot larger: the greatest United Airlines commercial of all time will have trouble convincing me to fly United. I'll get on a United plane only if it's like the only airline going at the moment; I don't like to fly United because they once did a job on my baggage that you wouldn't believe. Fortunately this kind of foul-up is on the ground.

All the great advertising in the world can never straighten out the stewardess who wakes up cranky one morning. There is nothing in the world an agency can do about the gas station attendant in One Horse Stand, Nebraska, who has a hangover. An agency can try to help with better dealer programs. Maybe. Or take TWA. They obviously felt that this customer-relation problem was enough of a headache to go out and run a campaign offering a million dollars in bonuses to its employees for being nice and polite.

The TWA campaign was excellent. First of all, the million dollars in prizes going to the nice TWA people comes out of the advertising budget. This is absolutely nothing when you're spending something in the neighborhood of $20 million. Second, the campaign probably cheers up these people working for TWA; it makes me feel that the people are going to be working harder.

Wells, Rich, Greene is doing the TWA campaign and it's interesting because the same campaign was to be presented to Avis, but they never saw it. An art director at Doyle, Dane came up with the campaign, the idea being that he was going to spend less money on advertising and more money in getting the Avis people to work. They'd give out bonuses and so forth. But the campaign never got out of the agency to be shown to Avis. The art director who had the idea was not the top art director on the account so the notion was kind of pushed off to the side. Mary Wells had the same idea and turned it into a multimillion-dollar campaign.

The idea has to work. It's just too good not to. It's got all the elements of a good campaign: it's amusing, it's got a good commercial situation around it and it gives people a reason why they can expect good service on TWA. You can't help but think something good is going to happen on TWA the next time you fly with them. And you've got the best of all possible worlds when you get your employees to back up your campaign. Forget all that crap about wearing little buttons. Here your employee is actually taking part in the campaign, and when the employees of a service organization *feel* they're important, it's everything. If you can get somebody at TWA to smile and act pleasant just because it's part of this whole thing and she feels like she's part of something, you've got a great campaign going for you.

Great campaigns that reach down to the employees of an organization are very rare. 'We Want You to Live' from Mobil reaches all the way down. Avis and Hertz do, too. When Avis said, 'We're number 2, we try harder,' the people who worked for Avis responded very well. Research was done at the time, and it showed that the Hertz people were actually affected by the Avis campaign. They found that the

Hertz employees were feeling low and deflated. Here Avis is jabbing away at them, and the company they work for is running commercials showing a crazy guy who flies into the front seat of a convertible. Norman, Craig & Kummel were the inventors of that flying fruitcake, and when Avis started hammering away, Hertz pulled the account out of Norman, Craig and gave it to Carl Ally. It wasn't that easy for Ally, either. He had to come up with what essentially is a very unpopular notion: taking on a guy head to head who admits he is second. And of course he also had the employee problem as well. The Hertz people felt rotten, and here was this aggressive young competitor coming up on the outside.

What Doyle, Dane had done for Avis was take a concept that had been around for years: You know, we're not as big as the next guy but we do a lot more. Nobody had ever quite crystallized this concept into 'We're number 2, We Try Harder.' I've done ads for Univac that said basically the same thing, trying to use the notion of Univac versus IBM, but not as well. Everybody's always got a situation where they're second but nobody had ever come right out and said it point-blank. And that's the difference between a so-so campaign and a great campaign.

In my opinion, one of the agencies that consistently produces superior campaigns is Leo Burnett. The interesting thing about Leo Burnett is, first of all, he must be seventy-five years old. So immediately he's not some long-haired kid. Second, his agency is in Chicago, and Chicago is really not major league. What makes him so brilliant is that he's got his roots in the Middle West. He's an ex-newspaperman and he really knows the people, he knows how people think, and he knows what makes people go. He produces very simple advertising, so simple that it's deceptive. You almost think it isn't good. It isn't sophisticated, and it doesn't make you laugh. But boy, it sells goods.

Burnett is the agency that figured out a way to sell vegetables: they invented this green eunuch called the Jolly Green Giant. The giant stands for great quality and he comes from the Valley of the Green Giant and the people look at this big green guy and figure, 'Gee, it's got to be good stuff.' And they buy. Who knows what the Green Giant stands for? Maybe because he's so big he means quality. If I had a product to market in the Middle West, I would go right to Burnett. Burnett even tells people what a corny agency he has, but he's not corny. He is a very brilliant man. That big green son of a bitch, that Jolly Green Giant, is fantastic. He sells beans, corn, peas, everything. When you watch the Jolly Green Giant, you know it's fantasy and yet you buy the product. Do you know what Libby does? I don't. Do you know what other food advertising is? I don't. Most food advertising is like gone by the boards, you don't even see it. But the Jolly Green Giant, it's been automatic success when he's on that screen.

For years Marlboro cigarettes had a selling line something like 'escape from the commonplace.' The advertising was fourth-rate. Burnett got his hand on Marlboro and went out and signed up a bunch of very masculine, very rugged guys and did a great campaign about the Marlboro Man. Now most of these were genuine rugged guys, not masculine-looking fags. He sold the daylights out of Marlboro. Then he switches from the Marlboro Man to Marlboro Country. Everything Burnett touches works. It's not the way I might do it, but boy, it sells the hell out of the product. Marlboro is now ranked around third of all the cigarettes in the country.

Burnett has a knack for finding a category of people to sell a product to. Another example is Virginia Slims cigarettes.

Burnett decided to direct his pitch to one group – the liberated woman. This doesn't mean that other groups won't be influenced, but the direct appeal of his message is to only one group. Virginia Slims are telling women, 'You've come a long way, baby,' and do you know what? A woman has been dying to hear somebody tell her that. She really secretly feels that she has come a long way, and it's a good, sexy campaign, a very good campaign, and great thinking. Burnett also sells cake mixes like nobody sells cake mixes. The Pillsbury advertising is great, great stuff. My wife sits there and looks at those ads of chocolate cakes and decides she wants to go out and learn to bake. He has an ability to really hit the consumer where he lives. Maytag appliances. You know, here's a shot of Mrs. Clancy and her thirteen children – and Mrs. Clancy looks like she's been through the dryer herself after those thirteen children – but there she is in an ad and she's saying that she couldn't have survived Mr. Clancy or the thirteen kids without her Maytag dryer which is still working. I mean, I don't care who you are, that's bound to sell. It also helps immeasurably that Maytag is a first-rate product with good word-of-mouth about it.

There is a tremendous creative revolution going on today in advertising. But the Bernbachs, the Rosser Reeveses, the Leo Burnetts, the Mary Wellses, despite their outward differences, are really not all that different. Different in execution but not different in basic premise.

Take Rosser Reeves, an authentic genius. His method of execution is to discover one thing about the product that you can make hay out of. Then you zero in on it and you make a lot of noise about it, forgetting everything about the product except this one unique selling proposition.

The key is to find out which button you can press on every

person that makes him want to buy your product over another product. What's the emotional thing that affects people?

The advertising that I had to do for Pretty Feet is a good example. My thinking was that people feel all their lives that they hate their feet – they're ugly, they're crinkly, they're embarrassing. I figure the average woman goes into a shoe store and she's so embarrassed by her feet that she twists them underneath her. The salesman's got to see them in order to fit her for the pair of shoes, and she doesn't even want him to see her feet. That to me is the key to selling Pretty Feet.

The execution might be different. My ad might say, 'What's the ugliest part of your body?' – which is a bit of a street-corner wise guy talking. David Ogilvy might say, 'Twelve ways your feet can look better.' Leo Burnett would have his Sally Claussen of Omaha, Nebraska, saying, 'I couldn't stand my feet for the first thirty years of my life but now I've found this wonderful thing that made them beautiful.'

When I was at Daniel & Charles, we always had a bit about how different agencies would answer their telephones. It shows you what I mean by the difference in execution. When you called Bates, they would answer by saying, 'Hello, Ted Bates, Hello Ted Bates, Hello Ted Bates.' Doyle, Dane would answer, *'Guten Morgen*, what can we do for you?' and PKL would say, 'Papert, Koenig, Lois. Fuck you!' In the old days Papert, Koenig was always a little hostile.

CHAPTER EIGHT
FIGHTS HEADACHES THREE WAYS

'The average copywriter and
art director never stop learning.
You have to know your product
so well you could go out and be a
salesman for the company pushing
the product. What you're trying
to do in all of this is to isolate the
problem of the company – naturally
they wouldn't have switched
their advertising to your agency
if everything was going along
fine. What you're trying to do is to
crystallize the problem. Once you
arrive at the problem, then your job
is really almost over, because the
solving of the problem is nothing.
The headache is finding out what
the problem is . . .'

I know that a lot of people are talking about this so-called creative revolution in advertising. *Newsweek* magazine did a cover story on the subject last summer. But it's interesting that when we talk about the creative revolution we don't talk about the great creativity which has been part of advertising for decades. There's a book out with one hundred of the greatest ads ever written and I would love to have written every one of them. Some of those ads go back to 1901. One of the ads is a tiny classified that says simply, 'We're looking for men who are willing to give up their lives.' The whole story was that an expedition was being planned to go to the Arctic, and the guys behind the expedition said, 'We're looking for men who are willing to go out on an adventure of a lifetime, but they may die on this great adventure.' Or get frostbit. A hell of a good ad.

Creative revolution may be an awkward way of saying there is good advertising and then there is garbage. It's always been that way. Today, of course, you've got some pretty strange kids turning out advertising, so for lack of a better name for these kids you could call them creative. Clients today really aren't aware of the extent of the weird behavior in agencies. They don't know about the real loose nuts in the agency. Agencies keep these guys in closets during presentations; otherwise a guy is going to show up high or he's going to do something pretty silly. The average client doesn't get to see the real weirdos; he'll get to see a guy he might *consider* weird, and by his standards is weird, but this guy is not agency-weird.

You take this guy Herb I had working for me, the fellow who wanted to own a live alarm clock. He wrote ads and commercials when the city was trying to pass a bond issue to improve the commuter railroads. One of the commercials showed what looked like a thousand people being pushed into a commuter train. That commercial was done from the point of view of the poor commuter. You could feel from that commercial how a guy like Herb could relate to the whole commuter problem. He works best on problems that are problems to most people. Nobody could know the little man better than Herb, because Herb is a little man who is concerned with the problems of life. He's close to it. He knows what it's all about. He can really feel and really relate to the consumer.

You can see a lot of Herb's personality coming out in his advertising and he's not unusual in this respect. A lot of people's personalities show up in their ads. I was once turned down for a job when I was starting out by a guy who said, 'You write like a street-corner wise guy.' At that time, it could be that there was hostility in my copy and it showed through – and maybe I still do write that way, though I like to think my hostility quotient is way down.

Evan Stark once wrote an ad for an air conditioner that took place in hell. You know, this is hell, and the devil gets all the bad guys and shoves them in a room and turns off the RCA Whirlpool air conditioner. That's what Evan felt hell was. The devil turns off the air conditioner. But this is Evan's personality. He feels and believes this sort of stuff. And that's what makes him such a great writer.

Guys like Charlie Moss and George Lois and even Ron Rosenfeld see things a lot differently from the average guy. I caught a real wild commercial the other day, a crazy thing with a car talking. Now how could a guy come up with a talking car in a commercial? Well, the chances are it was written by a copywriter who talks to cars – you know, he believes that cars do talk and if you talk to a car the car will talk right back.

All these strange guys eventually produce. At four o'clock in the morning, Herb was a fantastic writer. His personal problems never showed up in his advertising, but his personality did. I can sit and look at commercials and ads and tell you who wrote them. Guys who are wigged out write wigged-out stuff.

The giant accounts – they don't care about the craziness. All a General Foods worries about is the bottom of the line. The bottom of the line as far as they're concerned is that a guy showed up with an ad. The fact that it was done by a psychotic doesn't mean anything to them. They couldn't care less who did it. You could throw some copy and artwork into a machine, and if an ad came out they would be happy with it. The loose nuts are the problem only of the agency president who has to put up with them. Naturally it's a strain. I had a guy come into my office one day and tell me he didn't like the way the sun was shining in his window. I swear this is the truth. I said, 'Did you ever hear of a shade?' He said, 'There's something wrong, it's bothering me and I want another office.' Well, people usually come in and say, 'I'd like to have a bigger office.' No, he had to come in and say he didn't like the way the sun was shining into his window. Loose upstairs. We had another guy working for us who would take maybe three or four weeks on one ad. He would sit there and order $1,000 worth of stats for an ad that eventually cost $400 when it was printed and finished. So I'm seeing a $1,000 stat bill, with hours and hours of time, that must have cost my agency $6,000 to produce and when it runs it costs maybe $800 to place so the agency nets $120. I had to get rid of him and one day he met someone on the street who said, 'You were fired by Della Femina, weren't you?' He talked the way he worked. 'They . . . said . . . I . . . didn't . . . work . . . fast . . . enough . . .'

Most of the loose nuts in town work for the boutique agencies, which is the derogatory term used when the large agencies want to put down the small agencies. As far as I'm concerned, boutique advertising is the new advertising. Someone once made an analogy comparing the problems that we're now having in our schools with the problems now going on in advertising. In advertising, just like the schools, there is a group of people who are threatening an establishment and the establishment is fighting the threat. Perhaps the only difference is that a lot of us don't want to burn down the place, but we are a threat to the established group, which is made up of agencies like Ted Bates, J. Walter Thompson, Lennen & Newell, Foote, Cone & Belding, Compton, D'Arcy and others. They've been here many years and they haven't been bucked for many years, and all of a sudden guys are starting agencies and they have the audacity to take business away from the establishment.

In 1969 I went down south and pitched a giant tobacco company and picked up some business. Ten years ago I couldn't have gotten into any place in the whole state of North Carolina. They'd have taken one look at me at the state line and turned me away as some kind of menace. This is what is driving the establishment crazy.

By definition, a boutique is small. The establishment says that boutiques are cutesie-poo, very superficial, very flowery. Their idea of what a boutique is comes from what their wives tell them about the cute little boutique they found on Madison Avenue. The guy running this boutique might be standing behind the counter without a shirt on, maybe just some beads, and in the mind of the establishment this is no good. So they sat around and tried to come up with the worst name they could call this new type of agency, and boutique was it.

Doyle, Dane, Bernbach grew too fast to get into the boutique thing. Just as the establishment was starting to call Doyle, Dane a boutique it turned into a department store right before their eyes and just kept clobbering the hell out of them. They don't call Mary Wells a boutique because she opened and all of a sudden she's a department store. The boutique is the call given to maybe twenty to twenty-five agencies.

But think about the boutique for a moment. It means you're going to be dealing with the man who owns the store and you're going to get a lot more service and a lot more attention from him. Second of all, the item you buy from a boutique has to be perfect, otherwise you would go to another store. It's as simple as that. If you're running a Macy's, you sell everything in sight – you sell high-priced, low-priced, anything you can get your hands on. The object of Macy's is to sell, and the hell with service; the object of a boutique is also to sell, but with a maximum of personalized service into the bargain. So the boutique stays open until 10:00 p.m. Macy's closes at 6.00 p.m. A big difference.

You might go to Macy's because R. H. Macy was a great merchant and a great salesman and a brilliant man who got everyone to think Macy's when he wanted to buy anything beyond five-and-ten stuff – but whom do you find? You find a $90-a-week sales clerk with aching feet. She is R. H. Macy. The same thing happens in an agency. People might go to Ted Bates because Mr. Ted Bates is brilliant, but they might wind up with the equivalent of a $75-a-week trainee writing the stuff for their account. Chances are if an account goes to a boutique agency, they wind up working with the guy who did it all – the guy who started the agency. The word boutique used in a derogatory sense is a misnomer, it's a joke, and it's wrong.

But the small agencies are going to win, no matter what they call us. We win unless the kids who are striking in the schools take over, in which case nobody wins. The establishment is talking to a dying generation. They're not on the same wavelength as the younger kids today. That's why they're in trouble. The establishment can't change, it can't give the people anything different, it can't make the turn. The establishment doesn't know what makes people think; they don't know what makes people go any more. That's where they lose it, that's where they blow it. They've lost their ability to tell how people go, how people move, how to sell them their bra, how to sell them their hair lotion.

You think an establishment agency could have produced a campaign for Love cosmetics the way Mary Wells did? Never. It is a brilliant campaign and the packaging of the cosmetics themselves is phenomenal. The kids like the bottles so much they keep them after they've run out of lotion. The campaign is talking to kids the way they like being talked to. The kids they've used in the ads and the commercials are hippie-looking. They're also very good-looking, and all they talk about is love. In one of the commercials the guy had longer hair than the girl. In fact, his hair was so long and so nice I almost identified with him more than with the girl. They're very love-conscious, love-oriented. The Love cosmetics are selling like hell and they've got a problem in that they can't make the stuff fast enough. Now maybe it's a one-year phenomenon. The cosmetics business is a terrific jungle. But the fact that Love is selling means that they've got good advertising. The fact that they might stop selling means that maybe the product isn't there. But right now they're selling, they're doing a good job.

What's happening in business throughout the country is

that these younger kids are beginning to work their way up in management. They're in marketing, in sales, in promotion, in finance, and in a lot of cases, they're running things. The president of a sleepy corporation who is in his late sixties and is trying to get to retirement without blowing an artery is not going to take his account and give it to an agency like mine. He's going to keep it at his establishment agency where it's been for, like, fifty years. The seventy-five-year-old chairman of the board who has been friends with D'Arcy forever, he's not going to switch agencies. But the next generation – they're ours, we're going to own them. The next generation belongs to us; they're all ours.

There is a great difference in the way ads and commercials are produced at the creative agencies and at the oldline places. Before Bill Bernbach, old agencies used to produce advertising by the assembly-line method. This method, by the way, is still being used at most of the establishment agencies. First off, in the assembly-line way, a copywriter used to type up thirty, forty, even fifty headlines. All on the same subject. 'Aspirin Does This,' 'Aspirin Does That,' 'Aspirin Is for You,' 'Aspirin Is Your Friend,' 'Aspirin Likes You,' literally dozens of these things. Then the copywriter takes his headlines and goes to a copy chief, who sits there and looks at them and finally says, 'All right, number thirty-seven looks like you might be able to work up into some kind of a concept. Number forty-three, if you change this word, might work, too.'

When Rosser Reeves was running Ted Bates every writer would have to put each of his headlines on a single sheet of yellow paper. Then the writers would pin their headlines to a long wall in one of the rooms. Then Reeves used to come by, almost like a general reviewing the troops. He'd have his big red pencil with him and he'd look at the yellow sheets and say,

'All right, that one. Work that up. You might have something there.' One guy might have 'Fights Headaches Three Ways' and Reeves would say, 'That's not bad, that's not bad. Work up that one.'

You figure he had maybe twelve copywriters taking part in this thing, with something like fifty headlines a copywriter, which gives you six hundred ways to fight something. Out of the six hundred Reeves might pick four or five, and out of those he would sit down one day and come up with his concept of what the problem was, using maybe one of the headlines as a hook.

That was Reeves. At other places the copywriter would sit there and type like a son of a bitch and then go running into a copy chief who would look at it and say, 'That's got some merit. Why don't you work on that?' When it was all through bouncing back and forth between the copywriter and the copy supervisor, they would ship it into the art director. To the establishment agencies, an art director is a guy who draws. 'He's our drawing guy.' So they go in to their drawing guy with a headline that says 'Fights Headaches Three Ways.' Maybe the copywriter has got a little scribble of how the ad should look. Now the art director is, first of all, chained to his desk; they don't want art directors roaming the halls at large agencies. So he can't move around too much. He usually is between forty and fifty years old but even if he's a young guy his mind is fifty. He's sitting there minding his own business when the copywriter comes in and says, 'Okay, here's what we did. We want to say, "Fights Headaches Three Ways" and I think we should show a big pill.' The art director says, 'Terrific.' The copywriter says, 'We got to have a layout by this afternoon to show to the creative director.' The art director says, 'No problem,' and he puts it together.

FROM THOSE WONDERFUL FOLKS...

It's in the hands of the creative director by that afternoon and that's it. There's little relationship between the art director and the copywriter. They hardly know each other. They meet once a year at the Christmas party and the copywriter says to the drawer, 'Hey, how are you? Boy, we really turned out some great work together this year.' But they don't really work together, they don't get to see each other. It's really not two minds working on the same problem.

What Bernbach did was put the art director and the copywriter together in a room and let the chemistry take over. He has a lot of respect for people and people's minds. I think he got the feeling that it was a lot easier to have two bright people sit there thinking about the same problem than to have one bright person using himself as a judge. When Ron and I are working, when we're really on and really good, that door is locked. Like nobody exists. That room is a different place. A crazy chemistry takes over and suddenly the two of you think alike. With every art director I ever worked with I reached a point where I would start to say something and the art director would finish the sentence. I would say, 'What if we said, "What's the ugliest..."'' and the guy would say, 'I got it, I got it!' Without going any further.

The client knows nothing of this chemistry, this process. Why should he? He should care only what comes out of that room. Most clients, I'm sure, think that there's a magic something going on. That if a guy is called creative the guy has somehow been touched by a special ray of light from the hand of God. People think the creative guy can do things other people can't do. Nonsense.

The big agencies today are buying the mystique of the creative man – the big phony mystique. They buy the mystique and they pay top dollar for it and they don't know what to do with it. Why is it that an agency can hire a guy who is so good at one agency and turn him into a stumblebum in their own agency? Because they think creative advertising is a mystique; they think it's some kind of magic.

No one knows what it's like. No one knows what it is, no one knows the feeling. No one except other art directors and copywriters have ever been in on the excitement. That's why when clients sometimes try to do ads by saying, 'Well, what if you had a headline that said ...?' they have no idea what the feeling is about turning out an ad and what it is to achieve that feeling. There are things that I might say to Ron and he'll say, 'Are you crazy? You can't say that.' He'll then say, 'But what if we did this?' And he'll come up with something that's completely outlandish, but out of that outlandish thing there might be like one tiny dot there that says, 'No, you're wrong by doing it this way but if you tried it this way ...'

The way the whole process starts is that the art director and the copywriter do a lot of listening. When you've landed the account you've got to go through a lot of bullshit. There's research and marketing, the account executive, the agency president, the advertising manager of the account – everybody gets into the act. Everybody has something to say about the problem. The account executive, if he's good, can help. He's there because you might forget something and he's liable to say, 'Look, did you ever notice ...?' He might come up with a concept for you. He's another body.

The research guy does it with numbers. He says, 'Look, the way I see it, nine out of ten people aren't drinking this product because of the tests. It tastes like hell.' He doesn't give you a solution, he simply gives you another aspect of the problem. You've got the account guy talking to you, you've got the research guy talking to you, and you've got the account itself saying, 'Well, I think our problem is that people don't buy our product because they're prejudiced against us because our plant is in Hackensack.' Everybody's got their own stake in what they think the problem is.

Now that you have listened to everyone, you have to get to know the account. This involves a trip to their plant to watch their widgets being made or a trip to listen to their sales manager or a trip to listen to their salesmen or going out on the road with their route salesmen or going into a store and asking a guy what he thinks of the product. It is the most concentrated educational process in the world. I can be a little bit of an expert on almost every business that I've ever touched. In other words, I can tell you how to make a polyester in your home if you're crazy enough to want to know. I can tell you how the gases are pushed through all kinds of things and are turned into spaghetti coils, which then turn into fabric. I can tell you what it takes to sell time for a radio station. I can tell you how to be a route salesman for a product called Moxie. I know more about the feminine-hygiene business than I should legally know.

The average copywriter and art director never stop learning. You have to know your product so well you could go out and be a salesman for the company pushing the product. What you're trying to do in all of this is to isolate the problem of the company – naturally they wouldn't have switched their advertising to your agency if everything was going along fine. What you're trying to do is to crystallize the problem. Once you arrive at the problem, then your job is really almost over, because the solving of the problem is nothing. The headache is finding out what the problem is.

Then you walk into your room. When Ron and I start working we ask ourselves, 'What's bugging everybody?'

What is it? Define the problem. Most copywriters and art directors close the door and don't mention the product for hours – sometimes days, if we've got a lot of time. We sit there and shoot the breeze. Maybe we talk about sex, maybe we talk about the movies. Sometimes the relationship is one of hostility. I've been in agencies where the copywriter and the art director were screaming at each other for two or three days. One guy says, 'Where the hell have you been? I can't find you.' The other guy says, 'I'm not hiding, I'm here. You don't like to work.'

I used to work with an art director, and his thing was to scream and curse for eight hours a day. Sometimes he busted up furniture, just to make things a little more exciting. I loved working with this guy because you never were quite sure what was going to happen.

One guy might say, 'Did you go to the movies last night?' 'Yeah, let me tell you about the thing I saw last night.' This guy used to talk for hours about the movies he saw. Another art director I worked with used to talk about his house – his mortgage, his termites, the crabgrass, everything about his lousy house in Jersey. In a way, it's like two-man group therapy. It goes back and forth very fast and you're never quite sure who said what. When Ron and I were at Delehanty we did an ad for Talon Zippers – the one with the kid from 'Peanuts' on the pitcher's mound with his fly open – and to this day we still argue over who did it. I insist that I came up with the idea; he says he did. And we're both not kidding; we both think we came up with the notion. The thing is you blank out during the back-and-forth talking and nobody can remember who came up with which notion.

This same process holds true when you're working up a television commercial. One guy says, 'How about we open up with this, and then come in for a close-up?' The other guy says, 'No, let's not have a close-up, let's pull back for a shot of the aspirin bottle.' The profanity, the screaming, the yelling, the carrying on, the drinking, all at the same time – it's one tight crazy little room that explodes, and it's a very exciting process. To me, this is what advertising is all about because everything follows from that little room. After you've got the concept, then you take a photograph, then you have typography, then an engraving, then research to see if the idea will be effective, then you have to find the right media. But all of this is dependent on what goes on in the little room. You don't need research if nothing went on in that little room. The greatest media buyer in the world can't help you out if a dumb idea came out of that room. You could have Michelangelo setting type for your ad but it doesn't mean a thing if there's no chemistry.

The big problem in advertising is how to put the right team of copywriter and art director together. You're talking about chemistry or even a wedding, and it's not an easy thing to do. It's usually the job of the creative director to match the talent up. Helmut Krone, who just started his own agency with Gene Case, was a star art director for years at Doyle, Dane. But he was feared. Some of the hottest copywriters of our time went into that room with Krone and folded. The problem with Krone is, as I've heard it, that he doesn't talk – but nothing – he just sits and stares. So the copywriters at Doyle, Dane used to go in with Krone and talk and talk and talk, and finally they're running out of things to say. During all this talk Krone might have shaken his head once for a few seconds. Two days go by and the copywriter comes out of there wringing wet, twitching like a son of a bitch, wondering whether he should have taken up something else, like selling Bibles.

In the meantime, Krone is just methodically sitting there listening. He doesn't go in much for the chemistry. He's like a father, or a doctor. He's really got you lined up. He's just sitting there staring at you. Finally, after three or four days, he might come up with something and when he does it might be brilliant. He is a great art director; his only problem is that he's tough on the nerves of the copywriters.

There have been copywriters who don't talk and there have been cases where both the art director and the copywriter don't say a word to each other for hours. They just sit there for three hours and not one word is said. At the end of three hours one of the guys sighs and says, 'What if we said, "Fights Headaches Three Ways"?' The other guy might say, 'Nah, doesn't sound right.' And they'll sit there for another three hours.

There have been cases where the male art director takes a look at the pretty young girl copywriter and he turns the whole session into a pitch. The guy is sitting there thinking of headlines. A lot of affairs in the advertising business have started over 'Fights Headaches Three Ways.' First of all, this whole thing is very close, very much like sex. Here's the girl's chance to see the guy as a hero. You know, he's going to solve the problem. They're now two people struggling against this big problem. He says, 'Wait, I'll save you – I'll save your job, your little one-and-a-half-room apartment in the Eighties, I'm going to come up with a headline.' 'Fights Headaches Three Ways.' And bingo. He's a hero. And sometimes, like heroes, he's rewarded.

Doyle, Dane has had some very strange copywriters. One of the strangest was a girl who developed working with an art director to a fine art. Her theory was, 'What does it matter where we do the work as long as we produce?' So she quit going to the office, especially in the summer. You'd see her and the art director lounging around Central Park. If it was really hot, the two of them would take off for Amagansett. They'd work on the beach and come back with a campaign.

When a team fails to come up with something, they might go to the creative director and ask for help. A good creative director can be a great source of inspiration: 'Hey, look, why don't you just concentrate on this one area? Maybe you can come up with something and you'll be in better shape than you are right now. Go back and try again.' Like a hung jury, they're never dismissed immediately – they're told to go back and give it another try.

Some of the larger agencies that have switched to the team method occasionally have four or five teams working on the same problem – an ugly business. This means that only one team is going to win. The other four are going to be rejected, which also means that they're going to go out and look for jobs that day. The winning team, of course, is going to feel happy until the next time. That's the team theory of Rosser Reeves – throw everybody into the dike when there's a crisis. If a copywriter happened to be walking by Reeves, he would grab him and say, 'Find yourself an art director and get to work.'

I can't talk too much about the importance of the copywriter and the art director clicking together. It's the reason why creative agencies are doing so much better today. Sure, an agency making a pitch for business can say, 'Come with us, we're a great media agency.' What do you place if you haven't got advertising? How can an agency say, 'We're research-oriented'? What do you research if it doesn't lead to advertising? All the account needs is advertising – that's what he pays for – good advertising.

There comes a time when all agencies are created equal

and that time is when Jerry Della Femina & Partners, which maybe is billing $20 million, has a four-color ad in *Life* magazine next to a four-color ad from J. Walter Thompson, which bills maybe $640 million a year and has thousands of employees. No consumer sitting in the barber shop is going to know the difference in the two agencies behind those ads. Media are the great equalizers.

We're as good as anybody in *Life* or on NBC. We've got it made. We're right up against them and nobody knows it. Nobody ever said, 'I won't buy a Corum watch because Della Femina isn't billing what J. Walter Thompson is.' They really can't beat us – except in the quality of the ad or commercial. And that's what the game is all about. They might have more research and more bodies and more media guys, but when we print an ad and they print an ad, we're equal. They can't use one dime more of their money to look any better than we do in *Life*. They can't buy better supplies because we all buy the same supplies. They can't buy better photography because we know and use these same guys with long arms that they do. They can't buy better typography because we all buy the same typography. They can't buy a better page because the media has to give you the page next to anyone else's.

They can't buy anything that we can't buy and that's what's been the revolution in the business: People have suddenly discovered, 'If I give it to Thompson or if I give it to Della Femina, the difference is what winds up on the page.' It doesn't matter how many people the account met, or how much agency basketball is involved, or how many guys show up at a meeting. Bodies. You can always call Central Casting for bodies. We can deliver a hundred bodies if that's what's wanted by the account. But bodies aren't and never will be advertising.

CHAPTER NINE

FIGHTS HEADACHES FOUR WAYS

'It really doesn't matter what you did before you got into advertising. David Ogilvy worked in a restaurant kitchen and he's done quite nicely since. The key thing is, how much do you learn after you get into the business and then how well do you tell the consumer what you've learned? This is what it's all about . . .'

You can get into advertising in many different ways. I got into advertising because once, many years ago when I was a kid, I was a messenger for the advertising department of *The New York Times* and I used to deliver proofs of ads to department stores on Fifth Avenue. Wherever I went – Bonwit, Saks Fifth Avenue – in any of the stores I used to see guys sitting around with their feet propped up on desks. I liked that and I used to ask people who these cats were with their feet up. They were the department-store copywriters. That's when I made up my mind that copywriting was for me. My father, Mike, was and still is a paper cutter for *The Times*, working in the press room. My brother Joe works at *The Times* in classified ads. I have an Uncle Tony working as a compositor there and four cousins there too. The Della Femina family has been supported by *The Times* for many years. In my family the natural thing to do was to go to work for *The Times*. I had a choice. In our neighbourhood you could work for *The Times* or become a longshoreman. When I decided to become a copywriter, the neighborhood wrote me off as some kind of freak. The Gravesend section of Brooklyn is not what you might call strong on producing copywriters.

I got into advertising in a pretty straightforward way. But I know a beautiful guy at Bates who, before he got into the agency business, used to sell holy water by mail. It must have been fantastic. You know, you send in a buck and you get your bottle of holy water from Lourdes. Authentic holy water, too. When the holy-water associations used to get together they used to talk about this guy – like one of their gods. In the holy-water field, anyhow. He sold a lot of it. He went from selling holy water and making miracles with holy water to selling Anacin. Not too far apart. He went into selling Anacin because it was more profitable than selling holy water. It's too bad he didn't think about selling Anacin plus holy water. That's terrific packaging! You'd wash down the Anacin with the holy water.

It really doesn't matter what you did before you got into advertising. David Ogilvy worked in a restaurant kitchen and he's done quite nicely since. The key thing is, how much do you learn after you get into the business and then how well do you tell the consumer what you've learned? This is what it's all about. When John Kennedy was alive, a friend of his was quoted as saying that he had gone to school with Kennedy and he was just as smart as Kennedy in those days. But when they graduated, he got a job and Kennedy kept on learning. He never stopped learning. After a while there was a world of difference between the two.

You learn, you have to to survive. The first thing you do after picking up an account is learn. When we got the American Broadcasting Company's owned-and-operated stations, we traveled to their five stations. We heard all their news programs. We talked to their station managers. We learned, learned, learned, until we were almost ready to drop. It was a cram course in broadcasting and the thing was coming out of our ears.

If you bought what the ratings said, ABC News was running third behind CBS and NBC. But even though they were running third, ABC did have some characteristics that were very exciting. They knew that they liked going out and scoring newsbeats.

After we listened to everybody, Ron and I sat down and tried to figure it out. A couple of hours passed, and then in the middle of some story Ron was telling me he said, 'What is it that we're trying to say? Are we trying to say that ABC's news guys are not as staid as Cronkite?'

I came back at that and said, 'Look, you know what it is? It's like *The Front Page.*' He said, 'I never saw *The Front Page.*' I said that the type of news they have on ABC is not unlike the type of news coverage they used to have back in the days of *The Front Page* and Ben Hecht and Charles MacArthur creating Hildy Johnson. It's not the white-glove school of news that we've come to know and accept.

I said, 'It was an era of . . .'

And he said, 'Oh, like an exciting kind of news, right?'

'Yeah.'

'Well, were there some people who represent that kind of news?' I said, 'Sure. Guys like Murrow, like Walter Winchell, guys like Ernie Pyle.' Ron said, 'Look, why don't we start using these guys? And say our news has been patterned after the way they lived and the way they went out and got news?'

I said, 'All right, fine. We'll use Murrow. Murrow's great because he used to work for CBS. Now we've got a little more interest. We can imply in the ad, "Although he worked for a competitor, we always admired him and admired that he had the courage to go out and cover the Battle of Britain the way he did." We admired him and now we'll take many of the qualities of his reporting and apply it to our news programming.' Now we've got the beginning of an ad.

Nobody's put pencil to paper yet. We're just talking concept. The concept slowly comes out that we're going to tell the world that we have the same kind of news they were doing in the 1930s and the 1940s. Ron says, 'Gee, that's it. That's our last line. That's the whole concept of what the news is, that we're an exciting news station. We go out and get the news the way they did in the 1930s.' And from there on, out comes a campaign. Out comes the whole business. It just snowballs.

Now then, if Ron and I do all of this work, how can we stand to pick up the ad, hand it to a guy who's an account executive and say, 'All right. Go out and sell this to a client.' Yet this is what happens every day. And this is the big mistake of advertising as far as I'm concerned. We're there, we're sweating it out, we had twelve ideas, we kept three, we know exactly what we're doing. And in the meantime we finish it off and we say, 'Here, go out and tell them that this is good and they should buy it.' Well, that won't work. At my agency, we go out and talk it up ourselves.

The outsider thinks that all you have to do is win the account and from then on everything goes smoothly. Not true. You're constantly selling to the account. True, when you get the account, everything is a little easier, but with each campaign you've got to sell it to the client. Each time.

The way we work there is little difference between the art director and the copywriter. We're almost one person. I can do the layouts, Ron can come up with the selling line. And you discard ideas, you get rid of them.

Last year I came up with what I thought was a pretty good concept for Cinzano Vermouth. Ron didn't think so. We fought over it for days. It came about after one of our talks with their sales manager who mentioned that all vermouth turned yellow after a while. 'Every manufacturer has lots of bottles of yellow vermouth that nobody wants,' he said.

'Hey, that's interesting,' I said. 'What happens when you have yellow vermouth? You can't sell it now. Does everybody have this problem?'

'Yeah.'

Later, back in our office, I said to Ron, 'You know, yellow vermouth is an interesting notion. I wonder how you could make hay from something like this. What if you date the bottles? What if you put a date on the bottle telling the consumer when it was bottled. You could tell the people that when the stuff starts to go yellow you can't make a good martini with it. You can throw it in food, you can wash with it, but you can't use it to make a martini.'

But Ron doesn't buy it. 'Bullshit,' he said. 'It's too hard to do.' 'All right,' I said, 'let's pull it down to its simplest form. What do you do? You put a little tag on the bottle with a date on it. No other problem.'

Back and forth the idea went, for days. Every time we'd pass in the hall I'd say, 'What about the dating of the bottles?' Every time he'd say, 'Ah, that's bullshit. It's a gimmick.' I'd say, 'All right, it's a gimmick. Let's present it to them as a gimmick. Let's tell them what we want to do is that we have a gimmick that we want to show them.'

One of the key things in presenting a campaign is that you should never pitch a half-developed idea because you're assuming that they can visualize what's in your mind, which they can't, and you're taking a chance on having a good idea killed right in front of your eyes. If I had gone up to the client and said, 'Hey, we'd like to date the bottles,' the client probably would have said, 'Ah, it'll never work. How are you going to do it? It's not practical.' But if you go to the client with a bottle and say, 'Here's the label with the date. Here's the advertising for it, here's the thinking behind it. Here's how it becomes advertising. Here's a radio commercial, here's a storyboard for a television commercial, here's what we're going to do' – if you do it this way, you've got a better chance of selling it. I've seen guys blow good campaigns because they got so excited about them that they presented them not fully developed. In the end, my idea for Cinzano got shot down by Ron. He finally convinced me that basically the idea was too much of a gimmick and we dropped it.

Naturally the pace of the meeting between the art director and the copywriter varies, depending on when the ad or the commercial has to get out. Just the same, the chemistry is fantastic to watch. If you've got three days to come up with something, then you can really take your time. Or maybe it has to be out in a half hour, in which case the whole thing is speeded up.

One morning last summer Ron and I had to have some advertising ready to show at nine o'clock in the morning. We both got to the office at seven o'clock and neither of us had any idea what we wanted to say. The subject was institutional investing, and we had to have a campaign ready to run in a magazine called *The Institutional Investor*. That magazine is read by guys who have lots of dollars to spend in the market. Our client was Hirsch & Company, the stockbrokers, and through *The Institutional Investor* they were trying to reach the guy who is working for the ILGWU who's got maybe a million dollars of union funds to invest in the market. He has discretionary power over a lot of money and the idea is to get him to buy his blocks of stock through Hirsch & Company. How do you talk to this guy? That was the problem.

Sitting there at seven o'clock in the morning we were really desperate, I mean desperate, because the guy is coming in at nine o'clock to see advertising and he doesn't want to know from anything else. (Creative people in all agencies work best under the gun. If you were to give an agency three years to do something, they would wait until the last minute to do the work. Ron and I always wait until the deadline.) As far as he's concerned he's to be shown a campaign and he doesn't want to know that we've been backed up and busy as hell. It's a funny feeling; what are we going to do? Ron and I always work up to the wire but this was the closest we ever were. Maybe, we thought, this will be the time when we won't make it.

Well, we started out talking about sex. Seven o'clock! 'How are you?' 'Fine, how are you?' 'Boy, did you see Norma walk by here last night? Wow, what a body!' Comes 7:30 a.m. and nothing's happening. Like at about quarter of eight I say, 'What are we going to do with this problem?' Ron says, 'Aw, don't worry. We'll make it.' All of a sudden he says, 'I've been thinking about it all morning.' We started feeling sorry for ourselves. 'You know, it's really a pain in the ass,' I say. 'You never can go home and like just think of nothing, right?'

Ron says, 'Yeah. That's interesting, isn't it? That you always think of your job. I bet these guys in the institutional investing business feel the same way about themselves. I bet they think that they're heroes the way we think we're heroes for being here this early.'

I say, 'Yeah, that's interesting. I'll bet they really think they're hot stuff because they don't get to go to lunch because they're working so hard. Hey, did you ever notice when you don't go to lunch you really feel better because you think you're working so hard?'

Ron says, 'Yeah, I know. I feel great when I'm working like a son of a bitch and I don't go to lunch. I bet these guys feel the same way, sitting there with their millions of dollars to spend, they must really feel like they're something when they miss lunch or they have to order a hamburger sent in.'

And I say, 'Hey, a hamburger. Remember that day we were working with that guy Dave and he ordered a hamburger and it got cold? Remember how proud he was that he didn't even have time to eat?'

Ron says, 'Yeah, what a headline – "The Glory of the Cold Hamburger." That could be it, the whole campaign. "The Glory of the Cold Hamburger." That was the concept for the entire campaign, not just a single ad. The ideas started coming right out of the concept. The guy shaving in the morning saying that he thinks about stocks even in the bathroom and like he's putting in a twenty-four-hour day. We know that we want to show the reader of *The Institutional Investor* a picture of a hamburger and we want to say to him, 'You know, we understand exactly what it's like. You've got too much money and sometimes you don't know what to do with all of this money and there are too many people depending on you for you to run out and have a big expense-account lunch. So you order a hamburger in and it gets cold and you know what? You get a big charge out of it. You really think you're hot stuff for eating this cold hamburger and you know, you're right.'

The campaign started to grow from the guy feeling the way he does because he works so hard. The fact that he doesn't get a chance to see his kids. The fact that he shaves and thinks about work. The fact that he hasn't eaten a decent lunch in months. One by one the ads start to come: 'The Glory of the Cold Hamburger'; 'The 24-Hour Workday.'

Ron is drawing like a madman at this point. Now, how do we tie it all together? Well, why are these people working like this? Why are they breaking their necks? Because a lot of people are depending on them. Fine. That's the whole thing. 'Call Hirsch & Company because a lot of people are depending on you.'

By this time Ron is drawing with one hand and lettering in headlines with the other. There are four stages in making an ad: a thumbnail, which is just a tiny sketch; a rough, which is like a thumbnail, but big; a comp, which means the headline is lettered in and the drawing is much more detailed; and the finish.

'How do you like this?' he said. 'We've got a nice shot of the hamburger, with a couple of potato chips on the side, and we've got a little piece of type.' I'm sitting there writing copy now, mentally, and also talking it out. The excitement in the room is fantastic. Now we can't sit down. We're jumping up and down because we've a deadline to make and now we've got it and we know we're going to make it. There is an electric feeling in the room and this is what this business is all about as far as the creative person is concerned. Ron finishes his comps at 9:15. The man from Hirsch showed up at 9:20. We had five ads ready to show him – five complete layouts with the headline comped in, the body copy roughed in, with a slogan line that they can live with and go along with forever. It was ready.

The feeling in that room between 8:30 and 9:00 is like insanity. Ron is drawing as fast as he can, throwing papers around, and I'm chattering like a maniac. That's when an ad comes together, this is how it happens. No one has ever written about it. No one's ever come close to describing what it is. They talk about it as though it's magic. There's really no magic, nor is it very creative. You know what it's like? It's like two salesmen sitting down trying to find a handle on how they're going to sell the car this morning. It's nine o'clock and the door's going to open, people are going to come in, and what are we going to say to get them to buy this car? That's really the whole thing. People shouldn't try to make it into a writer and an art director. It's two salesmen sitting there trying to figure something out and coming up with an idea.

When the Hirsch guy came in he said, 'What have you got?' We said, 'Well, what we have is, these guys all want to be heroes, right?' He said, 'Right.' 'And some of these guys,' we said, 'they really feel sorry for themselves when they work like dogs, right?' 'Right.' 'Well, let's do a campaign glorifying them for breaking their ass, making them know that we know that they work hard. It's institutional, it's long-run. It's not going to mean a guy is going to call up Hirsch and Company and say, 'I want you because you ran that ad.' It means that maybe he's got his choice between Hirsch and Company and some other schnook he's never heard of before, he'll vaguely remember that Hirsch and Company did something he was really happy with.' The Hirsch man took one look at the ads and said, 'I buy it.'

The campaign ran, and it has been one of the good, successful campaigns in this area because the guys it was directed at – they can feel for it, it's them, it's their life. Some of these investment guys have even called Hirsch up asking for reprints of the ad. They want to hang it up in their offices. 'That's me, you know?' they say. They show it to their wives and say, 'You know why I come home late at night? Here's why.' They want to frame it. People are like that. They really do react to advertising.

It's pretty easy to see how that morning would only work with Ron and me in the room. You couldn't let anyone else in there, like an account executive. They would get in the way, interfere with the process. And you can also see the ease with which the guys who actually put together the ad can take it to the client and explain the ad and the campaign. What happens in the larger, older establishment agencies is that you've got copy chiefs, associate creative supervisors, creative supervisors on top of the actual creators of the ad. That's where the trouble begins. These copy experts, unless they're actually doing some work, are nothing but judges and superjudges. They sit there and they tell you whether they think something will work or not. They've no more right to be in that position than some empty suit off the street. Who is to become a judge? What qualifies somebody to be a judge? Years? Or salary? Or desire? What makes somebody a judge? That's why we never like to judge other people's work at our agency. Nobody is judged as far as their work is concerned. Sure, if a guy doesn't produce anything or if he comes up with a number of campaigns that the client turns down because they're bombs, well, then you've got to fire the guy. But nobody is ever told you can't do this or you can't try that or you can't present such an idea. Everyone's got the chance to bomb out.

Talk about the craziness of advertising. Where else do you hire a star art director or copywriter for $50,000 or $60,000 a year and then attempt to tell him what to do: 'Okay, we're paying you all this bread and now here's what we want you to do. We want you to do this; you can't do that.' Figure it out; here's a guy who's making all this money, and he certainly should know how to do it and what to do. He's being hired because he's an expert. Yet agencies hire top people every day and then attempt to show them what advertising is. It's strange – and stupid.

What's even stranger is when an agency doesn't use two-man creative teams but instead they call these giant conferences where they have so-called creative meetings. These are a real study in insanity because it's almost like a real group-therapy session, but everybody's got a big stake in this group session. You've got maybe four, five, or even six guys at this meeting. You've got the big $90,000-a-year creative director who is not going to allow an idea to go through that room unless it's his. The first guy who tries to sneak his own idea through will be killed by the creative director. He'll kill because he cares. How could he accept an idea from a guy who's making $60,000 a year?

The $60,000-a-year guy may be a creative supervisor and his job is to come up with an ad that will make the $90,000-a-year guy look silly in front of all those people. Wonderful situation! You've got maybe four other people who will have to say something in the course of that meeting so that the creative director will know they are alive. They've got to hang on. They don't care if they say the wrong thing – in fact they're expected to say the wrong thing. But they have to be heard. They throw lines like, 'Why don't we try ... ?'

Maybe you've got an account executive sitting in. His contribution is, 'You've got to come up with something or we'll lose the account.' He sets the tone of the meeting. 'We're going to blow it,' he says, and they all sit around throwing headlines at each other.

Maybe if the problem is big enough or crucial enough, the agency president will sit in. He's always felt he had a flair for the creative ever since he wrote that fantastic term paper back at Dartmouth where he got a B-plus and would have gotten an A if the teacher didn't dislike him. There they are, smoking and drinking coffee and playing creative. The first guy to try is always the $90,000-a-year guy. If he can score a big hit and rout the troops early, he's got it made. So he casually turns to the president and says, 'Look, "Fights Headaches Three Ways" has been working very well for us, it's given us a very good share of the market. Now if we can say, "Fights Headaches Five Ways" ...' And the president will look at the creative director and always shake his head yes. Big-time agency presidents never say no. They're like the Japanese. Always shaking their heads yes. They mean no a lot but they always say yes. The $90,000-a-year creative director doesn't know how to interpret the president's headshake so he plunges ahead with 'Fights Headaches Five Ways.'

The $60,000-a-year creative supervisor has been sitting there all this time trying to figure out how to bomb 'Fights Headaches Five Ways.' He can't bomb it directly, like saying, 'You're crazy,' or he'll lose his job. So the way he gets the supervisor is not calling the headline bad; he simply says it's not good enough. He'll also have a good reason for not doing it, such as, Albert Lasker used it in 1932 for a similar project. For all he knows, Lasker wrote a headline that said, 'Leeches Fight Headaches Five Ways.' Nobody else knows what Lasker said. To finish zapping the $90,000-a-year guy, the $60,000-a-year guy says, 'We gotta do a Doyle, Dane type of thing. We're going to lose this account if we don't go Doyle, Dane. We have to come up with their kind of headline. What would Doyle, Dane say in a situation like this? I just happen to have . . .' And with that he reaches into his pocket for the sixty headlines that he chomped away at the beginning of the meeting. He goes on and reads 'some stuff that I think is really Doyle, Dane.' And of course it really is terrible stuff.

The $90,000-a-year guy, who has been zapped once but who is very tricky, sees that the $60,000-a-year guy is very vulnerable after reading this garbage out loud to the meeting. He says, 'Look, this agency wasn't founded on Doyle, Dane's style because we don't do that kind of crap. Leave that to those boutiquey guys to do. We're going to hit them with solid advertising. That's what they hired us for.' Score one for the creative director.

The president is nodding all the time. The account man, by the way, is turning white because he really can see the account pulling out after all of this nonsense. The flunkies in the room are acting as if they're at a tennis game: they nod their heads to the left, they nod their heads to the right. They don't know where to nod first.

The meeting keeps going on. This year, it's fashionable for one guy to say we got to have a Wells, Rich, Greene commercial, and then the other guy knocks that notion off as soon as he rings in tradition, the history of the agency. Maybe the president has an early lunch date and he's had enough of the meeting. So he might suggest a compromise. He keeps the radicals happy who want a little Doyle, Dane ethnic humor and keeps the traditional guys happy by suggesting, 'Oy, Fights Headaches Four Ways.' Or something just as silly.

Do you think I'm kidding? I'm not. I'm dead serious. This kind of thing goes on all the time. They held this type of meeting at Fuller & Smith & Ross many years ago when the agency was trying to get the Air France account. The $60,000-a-year creative supervisor was trying to impress the $90,000-a-year creative director, and they all were throwing lines like, 'What if we say...?'

Sitting out of the main line of fire was a poor guy making $20,000 a year and he knew eventually he had to put his two cents' worth in, even though all the other people would dismiss it. He was a copy supervisor of some sort, but pretty far down the rung.

He spots a break in the conversation and says, 'You know, I thought of something. Air France, like it's French. Why don't we say something like "Come Home with Us to Paris"?' The meeting stopped dead in its tracks; the line struck them as great. Before the meeting was over the $90,000-a-year creative director was spouting the line as if it was his. He started by saying, 'Let me tell you, that is a good concept because we could...' It was armed robbery the way he grabbed the line. The $20,000-a-year guy wasn't heard from for the rest of the meeting. He kept raising his hand – you know, he had scored something and he might be making $25,000 by the end of the year. The guy had a heart condition – he later died of a heart attack. But he really was dead at that meeting. They ran over him. Nobody wanted to know he was there any more. Everybody went for that bandwagon as fast as they could. The creative director, being the heaviest at $90,000, got there first. The $60,000-a-year guy saw what was happening and he tried to take a shot at the line, he was trying to score too, and he's saying, 'Well, it's good, but what if we took part of the line . . .' The creative director beat off that attack quickly. 'Look, nothing is going to beat "Come Home with Us to Paris."

The creative director moved so quickly that before the meeting was out, people were convinced that the line was his. Each time somebody tried to bomb the line, the creative director would say, 'I insist that this is the way we've got to go.' People thought he came up with the line, he was defending it so much. Well, they got the Air France account and then things were even bigger and better for the creative director. I've seen it in different advertising trade papers crediting the creative director not only with the line but with pulling in the account. That creative director was making maybe $100,000 a year and riding high. The guy who came up with the line is dead and gone. The creative director was a hero at Fuller & Smith for a long, long time, just on the strength of that campaign. The only thing is that the creative director knows who came up with that line. He knows that he didn't; that he had to grab it off some poor guy. He has to know this and very late at night that guy must shake just a little bit.

CHAPTER TEN
CENSORSHIP

'One of the biggest problems that all agencies have is the headache of censorship. There is simply no reason to it. Censorship, any kind of censorship, is pure whim and fancy. It's one guy's idea of what is right for him. It's based on everything arbitrary. There are no rules, no standards, no laws . . .'

Y ou don't spend $50,000 or $60,000 to make a commercial
and just put it on the air. It's not that easy. There are
rules and regulations and censorship. There is so much of
this that it's goddamn funny and stupid. Sooner or later
every commercial is passed on by someone. The National
Association of Broadcasters is the national bunch of censors
and they pass on commercials on certain sensitive subjects,
like cigarette advertising, personal products, feminine
hygiene products, and parts of the body like the belly
button. The National Association is very strong on belly
buttons. If you get by the N.A.B., then you've got to deal
with the networks, which have their own censors. And the
individual stations, they've got their censors too.

One of the biggest problems that all agencies have is
the headache of censorship. There is simply no reason to
it. Censorship, any kind of censorship, is pure whim and
fancy. It's one guy's idea of what is right for him. It's based
on everything arbitrary. There are no rules, no standards, no
laws. The problem is, the Code of the National Association of
Broadcasters changes every week; each week a new directive
comes out of the N.A.B. I don't follow any rules or standards
or laws when I do commercials because how can I? What is
O.K. this week may not be good next week. There are no rules.
There's only Miss Cheng.

Now Miss Cheng is a very nice chick – her first name is
An-Shih – who is about thirty-one or thirty-two years old,
and she is the lady whom you see at the National Association
of Broadcasters when you want to clear a commercial. Miss
Cheng sits in her little room up on Madison Avenue, which
is a strange place for a censor to be, she sits there saving
the Great American Public from being offended. She has
no stake in any of the commercials, no money stake, all she

wants to do is keep America clean.

Although Miss Cheng is cute as hell, I have had my biggest problems with her in doing commercials for Feminique. All right, Feminique is a feminine hygiene product, to coin a phrase. Women use the spray so they will smell nice around their vaginas. This is what the stuff does. But you can't come within miles of saying this in an ad or a commercial. So what we tried to do was get a movie star to endorse the product in a commercial. We tried everybody. Vanessa Redgrave sent us a letter saying that we Americans were crazy over our clean armpits and so forth. She said that she thought Feminique was just one more example of the American craziness about cleanliness. As far as the vagina was concerned, Vanessa Redgrave said women ought to use bidets, soap, water, and baby powder. I'm standing there looking at the letter, and it dawned on me that we're not going to be able to get anybody.

I mean everybody turned us down, everybody but Linda Darnell, and she's been dead for three years. I'm sure that if she was alive she would have turned us down. Finally, the word comes from one of those endorsement outfits that Dorothy Provine, the television star, would do the commercial for $50,000. There was much rejoicing in the agency when Provine said she'd do it. Even though $50,000 is a lot of bread, we would have the only commercial on the air that will be able to get past all the things that the Code says you can't say. You can't even mention sex but Provine is sex. You can't say attractive but Provine is attractive. My theory was that when the competition looks at our commercial and we really start to fly and take off in sales the competition is going to say, 'We've got to get a star too to neutralize these people.' I figured out as I looked around that the only star left for them

FROM THOSE WONDERFUL FOLKS...

to get is Arthur Godfrey. He's doing Axion commercials now, but I mean he's the only star left.

We shot the commercial out in Los Angeles in a big mansion. We've got a great photographer, a director, script girls, dozens of people running around, and we've got a lot of bread tied up in this thing. I go into this mansion, which must have had forty rooms in it, to talk to Provine, and when I saw her I almost fainted. She was under the hair dryer and you know, this is not a good place to talk to a lady because ladies usually look lousy under hair dryers. I went downstairs feeling very uptight and nervous. I mean, here we are with a crew of twenty-five people, spending $50,000 for Provine and maybe another $25,000 for the commercial, and what are we going to do?

Finally, the time comes for Provine to come down. And she's beautiful. A fag makeup man has put her together and made her into something. I started talking to her and I said, 'I want you to give this a Sandy Dennis reading.' She said, 'What's a Sandy Dennis reading?' I said, 'A Sandy Dennis reading is as though you were mentally retarded for the first eighteen years of your life and you just learned how to talk but you can't remember words too good. So you say things like "This is the first time I've . . . uh . . . ever done . . . a . . . commercial." ' I said, 'It's got to be natural, like Sandy Dennis, you know – fake natural.'

She did it and she did it very well. There's one part where she comes on and says, 'This is the first time I've ever done a commercial. It's about a product that I . . . ah . . . feel very strongly about. . . . It's a feminine . .' And she gave us a terrific Sandy Dennis reading. A marvelous commercial. Then our troubles started with Miss Cheng.

The offices of the National Association of Broadcasters are

very deceptive. It's like another business office. You walk in, and there's a girl behind the desk and you say, 'Miss Cheng, please.' And out comes Miss Cheng. She's very soft-spoken, very nice, and I don't know, maybe she's the brains behind the whole thing. Her title is Senior Editor. All I know is that I've never seen many people up there. All you do is show your stuff to Miss Cheng. She always talks vaguely about people in the back she has to consult with but I've never seen more than one of those people. She goes away, and then she comes back with some of the stupidest decisions I have ever seen in my life.

You usually go up to Miss Cheng with your story-boards – those cardboard things with the various shots of the commercial drawn in and the audio typed out. With the Feminique commercial Miss Cheng did such a job on the storyboards that she knocked two-thirds of it out. Miss Cheng says we cannot say 'It's safe.' But we can say 'It will make you feel safe.' 'Well, doesn't this mean that the woman is safe?' 'Yes, but you can't say that *it's* safe.' Miss Cheng also does not like the use of the word 'feminine' three times in the commercial. 'Is feminine good enough to use once?' 'Certainly, you can use it once.' 'Well, why can't I use it three times?' 'Well, when you use it three times you're stressing it' Plus: 'You're not allowed to use your competitors' name, even though you're saying something nice about them.' Plus: 'You're not allowed to use the phrase "feminine hygiene."' However, Miss Cheng is cheerful throughout. 'Good luck with your commercial,' she says.

You could, of course, shoot the commercial without Miss Cheng's approval but you can't put it on the air. Oh, I guess you could put it on any station in the United States which doesn't subscribe to the Code of the National Association of Broadcasters. There may be two stations which don't subscribe to the Code – maybe one of them is in a big market like Monahans, Texas (KMOM-TV).

So you go ahead and rewrite the commercial to make Miss Cheng happy and you go out to the Coast to shoot it and you spend I don't know how many thousands of dollars putting it together and then you take it back to Miss Cheng so she can screen it. She looks at it in her little screening room, nodding her head sagely, and then the next day she calls you up and starts to hack away. One of the lines that Dorothy Provine says is, 'There are a lot of other great products, but the one I use is Feminique.' Miss Cheng doesn't want the 'but.' The 'but' indicates that we're trying to put down the competition. Miss Cheng wants Provine to say, 'There are a lot of great products – the one I use is Feminique.' Miss Cheng says we have a line in the commercial saying that Feminique has a fresh, clean fragrance you couldn't get from a shower or a bath. Miss Cheng says that the line indicates – and this is the way she puts it – 'you still stink' after a shower or a bath. So help me, 'you still stink.'

We're killed again. She held us up, more problems, more hang-ups. It will go on and it's a never-ending battle. The more power the censors get, the more I will have to fight them. And it's a fight that the agencies don't win. Eventually we got the commercial on the air. We dubbed, we cut, we made a mess out of a nice commercial to keep Miss Cheng happy.

I ran into censorship again when trying to run a print ad for Feminique in *McCall's* magazine. Art Stein was the publisher of *McCall's* at the time and he despised the thought of feminine hygiene. We went to him with the Provine commercial, which by now had been completed and cleared, and we showed him that the same ad had been accepted by the *Ladies Home Journal* and the *Washington Post* and a lot of other papers and magazines. Stein read the copy, part of which said, 'Now that the pill has freed you from worry, the spray will make all that freedom worthwhile.' 'What makes you think the women who read my magazine take the pill?' he said. 'Well,' we said, 'we have a story that you ran in your magazine six months ago about the pill and pregnancy and the whole thing.' We showed him the story. He said, 'That's the editorial side. My side is advertising. You can't tell women that the pill has freed them from worry. I won't accept it.' 'Fine,' I said, 'we'll take that line out.'

'You have another line here,' he said, pointing to a line which said something to the effect that when you bathe, take care of the most important part of you. 'This line,' he said, 'about take care of the most important part of you – you can't say that.' I said, 'Well, look, I wrote the ad and I happen to think that that is the most important part of a woman.'

Stein got very red in the face and he looked at me and said, 'Mr. Della Femina, did you ever hear of the heart?' I told him that when I went to bed with a woman I didn't particularly look for the heart. He said, 'You are not going into my magazine with this ad; you'll never get into my magazine with this ad. The story is closed.' Boom. And he got rid of it. Since then, Stein has been fired and the man who took his place came up to our agency last summer asking if he could have the very same ad in his magazine. Censorship is just somebody's hang-ups. I was censored because Mr. Stein could not bring himself to believe that the women who read his magazine had vaginas.

Don't think for a moment that we're the only ones having trouble with the censor because of the nature of the product. Once, at Bates, they turned out a commercial for a toy company that showed a kid with a little machine gun on top of a mound of dirt blasting away at Nazis or whomever we're killing or fighting with these days. Maybe Vietcong. The commercial was sent over to the censor and the answer came back, 'This commercial is not acceptable to the Code.'

The account man says, 'Why not?' He's obviously very shook about their reaction to the commercial. The account man figures he hit somebody up at the censor's office who hates war and is trying to downplay violence on the screen.

Not so. The censor said, 'Well, it's obvious that the mound of dirt is part of the game.' The account man said, 'Mound of dirt? What mound of dirt?' 'The mound of dirt the boy is shooting from.'

The account man blinks his eyes and steps back. 'The mound of dirt is part of the game? How could any kid think that the mound of dirt is part of the game? It's just a mound of dirt.'

The censor said, 'Well, the kid will obviously think that it's part of the game since it's on the screen for the entire commercial and the kid spends his time on the top of this mound of dirt.' The censor feels that the kid is going to expect to be given a mound of dirt with every machine gun. The censor told the account guy that Bates had a choice: either give the kids a mound of dirt with every gun sold or they could run a visual on the screen during the commercial saying, 'The mound of dirt does not come with the gun.' The account man, who's a very bright guy, suddenly feels that maybe he's in 1984 already. 'What kid,' he says, 'is going to believe this?' The censor had an answer for that one, too. 'It's not the five-year-old we're worried about. It's the one- and two-year-olds who might be swayed.' The account man, just to make sure, said, 'For the two-year-old kids who can't read I must flash on the screen 'This mound of dirt is not part of the game"? The five-year-old, who can read, is going to think we're crazy anyway.' The censor said, 'Yes, if you don't use a visual, the commercial doesn't play.' So it was flashed on the screen for the benefit of the two-year-olds who couldn't read. Nowhere in all this did anyone say, 'Gee, do you really think we should have a commercial running which shows a bloodthirsty little kid killing a bunch of kids with a realistic-looking machine gun.' No, that's fine. Kids can kill and everything else. The whole thing was the mound of dirt. That's censorship at its best.

I mentioned before that you just don't have one censor, sometimes two or three. Miss Cheng is the N.A.B.'s censor. The network censor is usually a woman by the name of McGillicutty or something to that effect, who is over forty, a little heavy, a virgin and a professional virgin – I mean not just a virgin virgin. Her job is to sit and look and read and see as many commercials as possible; that's the only job she has. The only thing she has to do all day long is to look for filth. If she doesn't find dirt, she really didn't earn her salary that day. So her job, day in, day out, is to find dirt. When she gets up in the morning and she's having her coffee, all she can think of is dirt and garbage and filth. You know, was that a breast I saw yesterday in that commercial? Did I catch a leer on that model or did she smile? Was that guy in the shower showing a little bit of his hip? 'Run that back, please, I think I saw a little bit of hip.' That's the whole day and the life of these people. You can imagine how twisted they are at the end of the day. It's a crazy job they have. Maybe I'm trying to get something across in a commercial; maybe I'm trying to say sex in a commercial and I'm beating her. And she can't be beaten, she's got to find it. It's a great big game: she's got to find the little bit of hip, the leer, the eyebrow that went up, the dirt.

Take the Noxzema commercial with the great-looking blonde, the one in which the blonde is sucking her thumb very, very suggestively and she's saying, 'Take it off, take it off.' That commercial is very sexy.

Somewhere along the line an account guy did a beautiful job. He must have taken the commercial in and sat down with an over-forty censor lady and they looked at it. Now if the censor raised any doubts about the blonde sucking her thumb, what's she going to say – that the thing looks like fellatio on the screen? The account guy must have said, 'She's sucking her thumb. If you can tell me anything else that it might suggest, I'll be glad to take it off the air.' What a job! The woman obviously couldn't bring herself to tell him what she thought the commercial suggested. I am sure that's how it happened.

Most of the time, though, you can't fake a censor out so easily. Smith/Greenland, a very good agency, was doing a commercial for Fresh, which is a deodorant. Why is it such clean products have such big troubles? Anyhow, they got past Miss Cheng, I mean they showed Miss Cheng what they wanted to do and she said, 'Terrific.'

They wanted to picture a belly dancer at her work, showing that she leads a strenuous, active life. Of course this belly dancer is terrific to smell all the time because she uses Fresh, which, hell, I don't know, doesn't wear off even if you want to spend a night belly dancing. They cut the commercial at a great deal of money, and when Miss Cheng saw the cut she said swell.

They figured they were in. What they didn't figure on was the NBC censor, who takes one look at the commercial and says, 'That's a belly button. My God, you can't show a belly button.' The theory was that kids might be watching and would see the belly button. Of course the NBC censor didn't realize that when kids go into their tub every night they look down and they see their belly buttons. But no belly buttons on the air. Not good. Forget that every kid has a belly button. Forget that.

All of a sudden Smith/Greenland has got this expensive commercial and no place to go with it. The censor at NBC absolutely cut the commercial to ribbons. There was a great deal of bitterness on both sides. The people at Fresh don't need these kinds of problems and here's an agency that has spent a lot of money and has no place to run it. Smith/Greenland had shown the commercial in storyboards to a censor. Who knows? Maybe the artist didn't draw a belly button, or if he did, maybe it wasn't a real, live, pulsating belly button, which would have caused them to stop the commercial at that stage. Smith/Greenland lost the account and it must have been billing more than a million dollars. What's so sad about this story is that you really can't win, you don't stand a chance.

The answer is, no censorship at all. The answer is, if you do something that's really tasteless, you'll be off the air – I mean you'll be off the air because people will stop buying your product. Sure, there's a lot of bad stuff on the air. The guy with the hammers in his head. The guy with the transparent sinuses. Terrible. It dies, it will die, but let it die under its own power. Who am I to say that that stuff is tasteless? I happen to think that quite a few agencies in this city put out a lot of tasteless garbage. But I don't have the right to tell them, No, you can't do this or you can't do that. My feelings on censorship are very simple: I haven't got the right to censor somebody else.

Sometimes the client steps in and tells the agency the commercial is no good. But that's censorship by the guy who's paying the bills. A lot of clients don't want to see their products portrayed in a certain way. Lots of clients don't even want to be on the borderline of bad taste. But it's different when the client tells you to tone it down than when some third party censors you. Miss Cheng says navels are all right, the Mrs. McGillicutty-type lady said that navels are out. Meanwhile, thousands of dollars are going down the drain. Miss Cheng is not worried about money. She has no stake in it at all. As I told her on the phone the other day, 'If I could say feminine once in the commercial, whom do I offend by saying it three times?' But in her little world, three times is too many times to say feminine. Once is all that she can allow me. And I lose again.

There's a classic Lenny Bruce bit. He's doing a father talking to his son while they're both watching a pornographic film. Bruce says, 'Son, I can't let you watch this. This is a picture of a couple making love and this is terrible and dirty and disgusting. Son, I'm going to have to cover your eyes now. That man is going to kiss that woman and they're going to make love and there's going to be pleasure and everything else and this is terrible, it's not for you to see until you're at least twenty-one. Instead, son, I am going to take you to a nice war movie. We certainly can go see a John Wayne war picture where there's blood and guts and killing and everything else. Because somebody's decided you can see that, son.'

If you're doing cigarette commercials, forget it. You can't say anything on cigarette commercials. Nothing. You're allowed to have a fag run up and down for a while in your commercial but he's not allowed to have fun in a cigarette commercial. Characters can't look like they're having fun.

They can't be endorsed by an athlete, can't be endorsed by anyone. Characters can't be too young and they can't look too bright. Right now, cigarettes are vulnerable. Who can't be a hero by not knocking cigarettes? The cigarette fight is really the most hypocritical form of censorship going – worse than Miss Cheng or Mrs. McGillicutty.

It's very hip to attack advertising right now and we're vulnerable because we're so segmented. Someone can get up in Congress and say, 'Well, the money that's being spent on selling soap could be spent on saving Harlem.' Everyone will agree to that except those people who are concerned with the making of and selling soap. It becomes easy, or seemingly easy, for a politician to swoop down and attack, but very few of them are so dumb as to attack advertising as a whole. Listen, politicians are some of the greatest advertisers going. Rockefeller – spends a fortune on advertising every time he runs for office. Javits – shrewd as hell. Treats himself like a product. When he takes a look at the surveys during a campaign and sees he is winning by a big margin, he's like any other advertiser – he simply cuts back on his advertising.

Senator Gaylord Nelson of Wisconsin held some hearings a couple of years ago and decided that U.S. tire makers of this country should spend less money on advertising and take that money and build a better tire with the money they saved by not advertising. He was saying they should cut the hell out of their advertising budgets. On the surface this sounds fantastic. As far as I'm concerned, if the tire manufacturers could make a better tire, they certainly would, because it would be a hell of a lot easier to market. But Nelson says they're spending too much money on advertising. I wrote a column in *Marketing/Communications* about Nelson and I happened to find out how much money he spent on his last Senatorial campaign. This politician who is yelling at the tire people spent – and it's a matter of public record at the State Capitol in Madison – spent like $486,338.34 on advertising himself in his last campaign. All right, why doesn't he cut down on his advertising and maybe use the money to make a better Senator? Maybe he could spend the money on hiring experts to cram him full of knowledge. He could do a lot with that money. What this country needs are more great Senators and Nelson ought to divert some of that ad budget into building better Senators. I could even write a pretty good campaign for him on that concept.

What the politicians use is the salami technique: they attack one group at a time. Now it's the cigarette companies' turn, next time maybe it'll be the drug guys again, and then the cars. They'll get down to the soap guys eventually. Just watch. When somebody tries to stop them their rationale is, 'Look, it's only one slice of this great business and we're doing it for your own good.'

The salami technique also has been used in truth in advertising and packaging. The U.S. Government has decided that you cannot call your cherry pie cherry pie unless it has thirty-two cherries per pie, or something like that. Now who's going to yell about the cherry pie? Not the bread manufacturers – they don't care. The bread guy is sitting there saying, 'Good for them, you show 'em, those bastards should do something about the cherries in their cherry pie.' The guy down the block who's making cigarettes, he doesn't care: 'Serves those guys right, it's about time they got after those bums who're selling cherry pie.'

The cherry-pie manufacturer, he gets it full force. Because one man in Washington has arbitrarily set a figure of cherries per cherry pie, the pie company comes up with an instrument that measures exactly the number of cherries per pie. It's almost like a sieve used in panning for gold. They dip this thing into a vat of guck, they sift it, and when the other guck falls through they've got to be able to count thirty-two cherries. Before they turn the sifter into the pie, they've got to have a minimum of thirty-two cherries in it. The Government feels that the average guy who digs into his cherry pie doesn't have any protection if he doesn't have enough cherries in the pie. The only person who gets outraged at this is the pie maker and he's doing it because he doesn't want to have to say that he has 'cherrylike' pie instead of 'cherry' pie. So he's going to comply with the ruling. Down the block another guy is thinking, 'Good. Get that cherry-pie bastard.' Nobody's together on this thing.

The Government goes on the theory that my wife or your wife or everybody's wife is too dumb to know the difference between the supercan and the monster can. That's their theory: We better take care of the people because the people are too stupid to watch out for themselves. What happens is that we get people like Bess Myerson or Betty Furness to watch out for us. It's amazing the people they recruit to be watchdogs for the people. I'm waiting for Frances Langford, or maybe Dorothy Lamour. Gloria De Haven would be good, too. Or Ann Miller. I can see Ann Miller doing twenty minutes on truth in packaging. I can't understand how the thing is so screwed up. Why do they go to the entertainment world? How about Mickey Rooney? Or Shirley Temple? No, she's out, because she's representing us at the UN.

What gets me really mad is that the Government gets so hypocritical about the whole business. The Government says cigarettes are a hazard to your health. O.K. Why don't they make the sale of cigarettes illegal? It would be very simple, no trouble – just classify cigarettes along with grass, heroin, hash, and whatever. Make them illegal. Well, I think the Government can't see its way clear to making them illegal because there is one hell of a lot of tax money coming in to the Government on the sale of cigarettes. The Government is making a lot of money on cigarettes right now – and who knows what the state and local governments are making on their taxes? The Government is a beneficiary of cigarette advertising. And this is the double standard.

The networks' giving up cigarette advertising is a joke. The networks are saying, 'Right, no more commercials.' But the reason is simple economics. The pressure had been great on the stations to run the American Cancer Society freebies. They've had to give up so much time from their programs that it no longer becomes economically feasible for them to continue to carry cigarette advertising. The networks can't keep carrying cigarette advertising and then give equal time to the anti-cigarette advertising and still stay in business. To get out of this bind, they're giving up the cigarette business.

If advertising agencies are such seducers, if they sway so many people to buy cigarettes, how come they can't sway people to stop smoking with anti-smoking campaigns? You either have a right to smoke or you don't. Either make it illegal or leave it alone. But enough of the double standard. Grass is illegal. Doctors are saying that maybe it's dangerous, maybe it isn't. The Government is sure – they say it's illegal, and depending upon where you are you can be put away for a long time for using it or selling it. In 1969 they held a rock festival at Bethel, New York, and like 400,000 kids sat out in a field and got stoned. Strictly illegal, and one sheriff said there weren't enough jails in three counties to hold all those who were smoking grass so they said the hell with it. Double standard, just like prohibition.

What the cigarette people did was to hire their own censor. They felt it would be easier to hire a guy to censor them now even more than the Government ever could. So they went out and hired Robert Meyner, formerly Governor of New Jersey. And the industry tells Meyner, 'Censor us. Keep us from doing things that the Government will get mad at.' He went so far that he's censoring them now even more than the Government ever could.

A friend of mine said to me not long ago, 'I'm going to beat them. I've got to get a cigarette commercial on the air.' Finally he came up with an idea. He would get the rights to the '59th Street Bridge Song' which has a line in the lyrics that goes 'feeling groovy,' and he would show a guy and a girl walking through Manhattan, smoking, and in the background, 'Feeling Groovy.' The Code said no good: 'Feeling Groovy' is a young song. It's young music. Get some older music. My friend was dead, finished.

Do you remember the famous ads made by Colonel Elliot Springs for Springmaid sheets? Lewd, tasteless stuff. He would have an Indian maiden with her dress up to her belly button and next to her would be an Indian guy. It was obvious that they had just finished screwing around. If you couldn't figure that out for yourself, the headline helped you out: 'A buck well spent on a Springmaid sheet.' You don't see that any more. In the end, the public killed it. They decided not to buy the sheets. Eventually tasteless advertising doesn't work, and there's no percentage in trying it.

The people kill bad advertising in a very good way. They don't write too many letters to the manufacturer; they just don't buy the product. All of a sudden you look around and you see sales dropping right before your eyes. The letters that the networks get are few and far between, as far as commercials are concerned. But when companies or networks do get letters, they get very uptight. I could control the entire advertising business with five little old ladies and five pens. All a company has to do is get more than twenty letters on a single commercial and it's out, it's dead. The company gets very nervous and the commercial is finished, washed up.

I once wrote an ad for men's socks and the ad showed a man standing next to a dog. I don't know why or can't even remember why we had a dog in the ad but it doesn't matter. The dog was there. Well, Kayser-Roth, the company that made the socks, got a letter from somebody in Ohio. The letter said that the dog is the filthiest of all animals and it went on to describe the habits of a dog – it was a pretty nauseating letter. But the letter got up to Chester Roth, the president of the company, and he thought enough of it to send it down to somebody, who thought enough of it to send it down to someone else, and it caused a little stir. Obviously, the guy who wrote it was a real nut. Four other dog haters could eliminate a lousy dog from an ad. We left our dog in but it was a close call.

The story that the censors put out is that they're doing it for the public good. That's all you ever hear about why they do it. They're going to ruin commercials, they're going to damage advertising, all because of the public good.

CHAPTER ELEVEN
RUMORS AND PITCHES

'The outsider who reads about this kind of infighting might be horrified, but strangely enough I enjoy it. I think it's a lot of fun. I like it when somebody zaps me. The guy who said we weren't taking small accounts did a beautiful job – he really got me. He put me in a position where I couldn't fight back and I can admire the job he did. The thing to remember about the entire rumor game is that you can't touch a solid account and you can't bother a solid advertising man . . .'

I once made a presentation to an account when I was at Delehanty, Kurnit & Geller. The guy who owned the company zapped us out. He was straight as an arrow, great-looking guy, big, tall, basketball-playing type. I ran into him about six months later on the ferry to Fire Island. He was with another guy and they had their arms around each other. As I walked by I caught him from the side of my eye and I said to myself, 'I really didn't see that.' So I kept walking, like I didn't really want to meet him and talk to him on the ferry. My wife was sitting in the front of the ferry and since he saw me alone he figured, Well, golly, here we go. 'Jerry,' he said, 'how *are* you?' I couldn't remember his name, I only remembered that we pitched the account. He's there, grinning, with his four buddies, and he said, 'Who are *you* here with?' 'I'm here with my wife,' I mumbled. 'Oh,' he said, '*Oh*.' That was that.

Now, if I had known about this guy when I made the presentation, why you can't tell, I might have done something to get an edge on the account. Like wear a dress. No, of course that's not true, but it is true that you work like hell to pick up the business.

Before you even get a chance to present, you have to know that the account you're going to pitch to is loose – that is, you have to be aware that the account wants to listen to you. You hear about possible new business through rumors. Rumors are very important in this business. Whether you start them or whether you're the victim of them, rumors are crucial to advertising. This is one of the few businesses where people are so rumor-conscious. You'll almost never find two lawyers sitting around discussing whether Sullivan & Cromwell is going to lose a client.

Rumor, gossip, whatever you want to call it, it's essential to advertising. People use the advertising trade papers to push their careers, make a pitch for an account, or to zap guys who have an inside track on an account. The most important trade papers for rumors are *ANNY (Advertising News of New York)*, *The Gallagher Report*, *Ad Age* and *Ad Daily*. *ANNY* also has a counterpart in Chicago and on the West Coast. People sit down and read *ANNY* and *The Gallagher Report* to find out if they're going to lose their accounts. *The New York Times* is the single most powerful force in the business as far as straight advertising news is concerned. *The Times* does not go in for rumors, just plain news, when an account finally moves from one agency to another and items like that.

The trade papers print rumors – on purpose – when the rumors come from a reliable source. One of the trades printed a rumor in 1969 that a soap company was thinking of developing an enzyme which would be competitive, really competitive, with another soap. The story said that if the company did bring out this soap they would give the account to a large agency, which then would have to drop their soap account because of a product conflict. I happen to know that the guy who planted that rumor did it because he wanted to be able to say to Soap Company No. 1, 'What's with the story? Is it true? And if so, we'd like to be in the running for the account that was to be dropped.' This was a legitimate rumor that went to the press, and who knows if something will come of it? You can't tell.

The press is of value to someone in looking for new business or in solidifying his position with an account. As far as I'm concerned the rumor business is not all dirty pool. It's like a race toward an account and everybody does everything in their power to get it. Agencies hire stars to impress the account, guys do anything to get the account. Part of the race for the account is the rumor. It's true that there are some bad people who immediately go out and try to kill the other agencies who also are pitching the account. They'll spread rumors that an agency's best people are leaving. There are cases when people will sit down and spread lies – not rumors that may have a basis in fact. A good example of this recently was the rumor spread that Doyle, Dane's best people were leaving for other agencies. Now Doyle, Dane was about to get a big chunk of business, and somebody spread this rumor about them so the account might think that it might not pay to go to Doyle, Dane if the people working there were leaving.

We in advertising really would be kidding ourselves if we didn't admit that the rumor business existed. Agency presidents use it: they put in a call to Gallagher and they drop whatever news they want to drop. It's not unlike Hollywood around the time when the Oscars are given out. 'Joe Whateverhisname is a sure bet to get an Oscar for Best Supporting Actor.' That's Joe's agent at work, planting rumors.

The trade papers check out rumors. They're not innocent victims and you just can't get them to spread anything that they can't check out. You can't buy them because they're not buyable. They're extremely careful to protect their sources. No one ever gets to know where a rumor comes from. You only can guess. You read a story about yourself in *ANNY* and you can't find out who fed it to them for love or money.

When we first went into business and we were having a hell of a time just staying afloat, a story appeared in *Ad Age* saying that two of our partners were unhappy with their setup and thinking of leaving and going to another agency. At the time, I just didn't want a story like that printed – even though it had a basis in fact – and obviously the rumor had been fed to *Ad Age* by somebody. I called them up and said,

'What's this all about? It's not so. Who said it?' And they said, 'Just as we would protect you if you were to talk to us, we have to protect our source on a story about you.' A rumor about our agency got into *Ad Daily* last year and all it said was, 'Jerry Della Femina successful. Will no longer talk to small accounts.'

Now that's not so. Ed Buxton of *Ad Daily* is a very good friend of mine so I called him up and said, 'Hi, how's everything? What's this I hear about me not talking to small accounts? You know, some of them pay a lot of money to come see an agency like this. You're going to turn off a couple.'

He said, 'Jerry, I've got to protect my sources. We heard that you've established a limit now on the size of an account you'll take, and that's it for a small account. We heard that nobody gets in unless they're billing such and such.'

What a beautiful rumor somebody fed Ed. Do I now come out and say, 'Jerry Della Femina & Partners announce that they'll take any small account they can get?' I mean, any kind of rebuttal that I issue is deadly for me – anything short of silence is no good. If I come out and say, Yes, I want small accounts, that will be read by people to mean that Jerry Della Femina is in trouble and he wants all the small accounts he can grab. The guy who fed that rumor was very bright – and I know exactly who it was – because he zapped me out of maybe ten accounts that might be able to bill say $150,000, $200,000 or even $300,000. Who knows what 'small' means? A guy billing maybe $1 million might say to himself, 'Gee, I'm not big enough for them any more. I might not have a chance.'

It's a very tricky business. Let's say that a new agency has opened up and they have assurances that the account which is loose over at the Joe Doakes agency is going to go to them. No papers have been signed, but everyone has agreed to the thing.

The account is making this move partly to take advantage of the big publicity that comes when a new shop opens with a big new account. Now ANNY calls guys every Wednesday, they've got a list of sources all over town, and they get on the telephone and say, 'What's new around town?'

They might call a guy who is familiar with the situation of the new agency opening and getting the loose account at Joe Doakes. And this guy they call might decide to zap the new agency and take a shot at the Doakes account himself. What he does is to tell ANNY that the big Widget account over at Doakes is going to leave and go to the new agency. 'It's too bad,' says the guy to ANNY, 'but that's what I heard. Why don't you check it out?' ANNY calls the new agency and asks if it's true that they're going to pick up the Widget account. The guy who is forming the new agency is dead. He has his head between his hands because part of the big mystique in his talking to the Widget people was, 'Well, we want you to be our first account and we expect it to make a big splash.' If ANNY prints a story which says that Jim So-and-So, one of the partners of the new agency, said there is no news to report at this time concerning the Widget account, the issue is dead. It's now a dead story as far as the business trade is concerned. With a dead story, the Widget people just lost the one big reason why they want to go to the new agency. Everyone had been saying to each other, 'Well, we would be their first account and we would get the full treatment, the whole splash, like, "They opened today and they opened with this particular account." ' With the news out it's not going to happen that way. What may happen is that the Widget people will say, 'Gee, this new agency must have blabbed it around about our leaving the Doakes people. What do we need with a bunch of bigmouths?'

The clients all read the trade papers, but very few of them realize the infighting that is going on all the time. All they know is whenever their name is mentioned in the wrong way they get upset. They don't know of the blood being shed behind the lines. I saw a story recently about an agency – and the agency was named – saying that they were doing some work for Carter-Wallace, Inc. The story said that the project 'is under wraps. No details available.' I don't know anything more about this story but I do know that somebody just got zapped out. An executive at Carter-Wallace must have seen the story and then called the agency which was doing the project— 'We thought that this was very confidential, and if it's not confidential why didn't you tell us that you couldn't keep a secret?' Somebody bombed the agency. Who knows why?

There are some agencies that just are not aware of what's going on. Day in, day out, these agencies constantly take it on the chin. Some agencies' guys are nice, sweet, warm guys who want to go home to Rye at night and they don't want to know from rumors. They no more know how to handle rumors than the man in the moon.

Very few people go around telling out-and-out lies in the rumor game – this is where you tend to draw the line. But if there's a piece of news, some guys use it to their best advantage. That's all it really is. People also draw the line at taking unfair advantage of a guy. They would not call up a trade paper and say outright that somebody's about to lose an account. They don't call up a paper and say, 'Hey, I've got a tip for you, baby.' Like that's bad news. They let the press call them. I once got a phone call from one of the trade papers:

'What do you hear?'

'I haven't heard anything.'

'Well, let me see if I can refresh your memory. I hear you're pitching National Airlines?'

'National? They're at Papert, Koenig, Lois. There's always talk about National Airlines. But I'm not doing anything.'

'Well, we hear they're really talking to somebody.'

I say, 'Is your source a good source?'

'My source is a pretty good source.'

I say, 'Fine. Why don't you call up PKL? They're going to deny it. Why don't you call up National? They'll admit it because National always admits these things. They always say, "We talk to agencies all the time."'

During that call I really knew nothing about National and PKL so I really couldn't help the guy from the trade paper. If I was pitching National I would have told him. But I don't think anyone with class ever picks up the phone to say, 'Hey, did you hear that . . . ?' I think that's tipping, and it's wrong.

People use rumors to zap out other people. An example of this terrible practice is the case of Mary Wells. According to *The Gallagher Report*, Mary Wells used to have only a thirty-day contract with her own agency. But people began to use this report against her and it was affecting her new business. How did the word that she had only a short contract ever get out? Who knows? But I'll bet she didn't run around town screaming it. Somebody leaked it from Wells, Rich & Greene to somebody else where it got to *The Gallagher Report* where Gallagher did a whole series of columns on it. Wells, Rich might be pitching an account and another agency also pitching the account might say to the prospective client, 'What do you want to go to Wells, Rich for? Mary Wells has only a thirty-day contract. She can walk out any time she wants to.' To combat this kind of thing she just signed a ten-year contract with her own company. Now, nobody can zap Wells, Rich with the line about Mary Wells leaving any more. A client can say to himself, 'For the next ten years I have Mary.' So she's set and she's going to do very well. But figure how nasty the business is when she had to sign such a long-term contract to combat the rumors. And of course, when she did sign, it made big news with all the trade papers.

Guys in an agency try to knock off other guys in the same agency by using rumors. I once worked for a place where the executive vice-president – a guy I'll call Hunter – was trying to zap the president of the agency, whom I'll call Duffy. Week in, week out, Hunter spread rumors that he was going to become president. Duffy was slowly getting zapped all over the place. The rumors were of the kind with the intimate, quiet business details that only the two guys knew about. Whenever anyone questioned Hunter about these terrible rumors he would shrug his shoulders and say, 'Who, me? I don't even know how that started.'

Hunter hasn't got the job yet. But he's going to get it eventually. Day in, day out, another rumor. You'd open up *The Gallagher Report* and you'd read, 'Hunter is going to get Duffy's job.' Or, 'Hunter is a good replacement for Duffy.' Or, 'Duffy is getting along in years and must be concerned about the National Clambake business, which isn't as solid as it used to be.' The average person reading this must wonder, 'Why doesn't Duffy walk into Hunter's office one day and punch him in the mouth?' That's not the way they play the game. Duffy will see Hunter and say, 'Hunter, how are you?' Hunter says, 'Fine, but I'm very upset by all these rumors about you. I can't imagine how they're starting.' Duffy simply cannot fire Hunter. Hunter has a contract and is well set up at the agency. He can't be fired without a meeting of the entire board of directors.

One day Hunter and I had to take a cab together on an appointment. He started, 'Jesus, I don't know how these rumors about Duffy and me are starting. Did you see the one today in *The Gallagher Report*?' I said, 'Hunter, cut the crap. I know where the rumors come from. You're sending them in.' He sighed and said, 'Ah, let's change the subject.' That was it, just change the subject.

The outsider who reads about this kind of infighting might be horrified, but strangely enough I enjoy it. I think it's a lot of fun. I like it when somebody zaps me. The guy who said we weren't taking small accounts did a beautiful job – he really got me. He put me in a position where I couldn't fight back and I can admire the job he did. The thing to remember about the entire rumor game is that you can't touch a solid account and you can't bother a solid advertising man. A rumor will start, the trade paper will call the advertising manager of the account, and the advertising manager will say, 'Shove it.' Take Talon Zippers at Delehanty, Kurnit & Geller. Talon is very happy; they're getting good advertising and they're content. They could start a million rumors but those people are not going to move. Rumors only occur when there is something wrong with the advertising being done for the account.

Rumors are especially heavy nowadays with the revolution going on in the business. The older agencies are slipping and they're getting desperate. Therefore, plenty of rumors. The younger agencies are aggressive and really pretty tough. Therefore, plenty of rumors. The guy in the older agency who is trying to hold on is vulnerable to rumors. He fights back by sending out a lot of rumors. All of this is followed by the young guy trying to build an agency who is going to make it if he has to stomp over the first ten people he sees. He's putting out rumors too, and some nasty ones at that.

A lot of people watch all of this carrying on and wonder what would happen if guys would quit screwing around with rumors and spend their time on advertising. The truth is, there's plenty of time to do both. I get a kick out of the rumor business because I look at it as part of the total warfare of the advertising game. Remember, there are all kinds of warfare. Suppose someone said, 'Why don't they just go in there with their guns and wipe out that town? What's this bit about psychological warfare? What's this bit about spies and everything else? You take your tanks and you go in and you take the town.' Well, maybe somewhere along the line someone discovered that there are fifty different ways to capture this town. You need the tanks and you need the guns, but then maybe you'll also need a lot of other little things that people don't even consider. It's part of the game, it's part of the mix. Publicity is also part of the mix.

I don't want to get too far away from rumors, but if you look at Doyle, Dane for a minute, you have to agree that in their own quiet, reserved, wonderful way they've done a fantastic public-relations job. There is no doubt about it, they're very public-relations conscious. Nobody ever gets the feeling that they get publicity. It just seems that they win things and they do things, and isn't it nice? They have a very good girl in charge of their publicity and they are very well buttoned up about what they do and how they do it. Mary Wells hired a girl to handle public relations for them. There is no such thing as an agency which steadily turns out such good work that everybody automatically looks up and says, 'Yeah, aren't they good?' It's public relations and a lot of other things.

Part of the rumor business is the way you make yourself accessible to people who are looking for a job. Let's call the getting and losing of an account a war. Let's also say that in a war the first thing you need for the fight is ammunition, and ammunition in advertising is good ads. Second, all the ammunition in the world won't help you if you haven't got information. Intelligence. Intelligence is knowing what's going on, knowing what the people are doing down the block. As far as I'm concerned, you just can't operate out of a vacuum. You just can't say, 'Well, I know what I'm doing so I don't have to worry about what they're doing down the block.' You'll never get an account that way; you'll never be able to pick an account.

I interview people – always – with an eye toward hiring them, but also I regard these people who come in for a job as the greatest source of information as to what's going on in the business. Some of the people who walk in are unhappy with their job or their agency. Others are trying to impress you with their knowledge of what's going on in their agency. They're ready to tell you anything – some of them just spill out at the mouth. I saw a girl not long ago – a kid in a media job at a good agency in town. In the course of one little interview she told me that the people at a very good account with her agency were very unhappy because they felt they were not getting the kind of service that they would like. The word she used was 'pampered.' 'What do you mean by "pampered"?' I asked. She said, 'Well, it's not that they want to be pampered. But they'd like to see the agency president come in at least once every two weeks to show them the ads and talk to them. They want to deal president to president.'

All right, now here's a piece of loose intelligence that has been handed to me. What do you do with it? Well, tomorrow maybe I can put in a call to the account saying it's about time that we talked – that we sat down and had some lunch together since I feel that one of the things which is making our agency grow is the fact that we're at the size where we can get together – president to president – and talk about advertising. Maybe I won't ever get that account but I do have a lead on $1.5 million worth of business and I know exactly what's wrong up there.

Agency presidents should keep their people happy. People have big mouths and they go out and blab, and an angry person has an even bigger mouth. The girl I was talking to also mentioned something about the president of her agency – the fact that he might be retiring. She told me enough about what's going on in that shop that I know right now that there are two or three accounts that are worth shooting for there, and I know what their problems are. This girl talked about one of their electronics accounts. And she pinpointed the specific problems on the account.

Now this is one girl. One job. Multiply her three or four times a day and you get to know exactly what accounts are loose or in trouble around town. I believe all of the newer and smaller agencies work this way when they're talking to people about jobs. But it doesn't work like that at the larger agencies. If somebody goes to ask for a job at J. Walter Thompson, forget it. The lines of communication must be so screwed up there because of Thompson's size that any valuable word from an interview will never get its way back up to the guys who pitch. Thompson is so big that if there was a fire there, a guy couldn't get the word to enough people to prevent a major tragedy. At a small agency, the relationship is one to one. Agency president talking to media girl, media girl spills her guts out, agency president makes the call tomorrow and possibly gets the account.

A Doyle, Dane is past the stage that they have to go digging for information. They're at the point where people call them on possible new business and they're not fighting hard. I get calls too, a lot of them. But I'm also fighting hard. Also, there's a Machiavellian thing to this whole business that I love, and no matter how we grow I don't think I'll ever sit back and say to myself, 'Well, that's it. I don't want to hustle any more.' I enjoy this part of it; I enjoy it almost as much as I enjoy doing ads and commercials. I get a charge out of finding information and then putting it to use.

Corum Watches is one of our oldest accounts and truly one of the best. Good success story for us. One of their watches is an old American gold piece split in half, with a watch movement inserted in it. We sell that thing very big in Texas. We heard about Corum originally from a guy at *Look* magazine who said they were looking for an agency and we ought to pitch it. After I got the call I got out the phone book and couldn't even find Corum Watches. I got back to the guy on *Look* magazine who knew the account. 'Sure, Corum, know them well. Guy by the name of Jerry Greenberg is in charge of the whole business. He really is a great guy.' I asked him about Greenberg. 'Well, Jerry is a Cuban refugee, and he speaks with a heavy Spanish accent. He's a very gentle guy, very nice guy, but he likes ballsy things.'

I picked up the phone, got Corum, and said, 'Hello, Jerry Greenberg, I hear your account is loose. I'd like to come in and talk to you about it.' At that point there's no sense saying we should get together and have a little talk. He's already talking to other agencies and I might have been too late. He had never heard of me. We had been in business for three months and things were bad. We were running out of bread, two of our partners had decided to pull out and things were very tight. I went to see him, showed him the stuff and got the account, just like that. I practically got it while I was there. When we took over the account Corum was advertising in the *Times* Magazine and spending something like $65,000. The account now bills close to a half million dollars with us. It's a major account with us – and pretty soon he's going to be all over the lot. His sales are fantastic – on that watch made out of a gold piece he's backed up with orders, two or three months' worth. The guy has a watch company now. When you're able to spend close to $500,000 in promotion and advertising, you've got to be making a lot of bread.

Let's say you track down a rumor and you're asked to make a pitch. You can do it two ways. You can have a standard regular pitch which you make to every prospective new client. Or you can do a lot of work on spec, showing the guy what kind of campaign he should have. Mostly the new and younger agencies feature a standard pitch. They don't believe in freebies – for anybody. The older agencies – the establishment, which is running scared – will do anything for new business and they'll go to any lengths, like preparing a whole campaign on spec. Like the TWA thing, which is the great example. One thing good that did come out of the TWA pitch was a growing reluctance on the part of all agencies to do free work.

There is still a third way to get an account, but it is really going out of style fast. What happens is that the chairman of the board of an old-fashioned big agency learns that an account is loose and remembers that he went to school with Bunny or Snoopie or whatever, who now is chairman of the board of the account. The advertising chairman of the board calls his friend at Chase Manhattan and the banker quietly sets up a discreet lunch for the two chairmen of the board. They have a terrific lunch, which is featured by the lack of talk about advertising. Maybe they'll talk about their mutual friend Stinky who was a big man because he stole the town bell one night after the senior hop. You've got to understand that the two chairmen of the board really can't discuss advertising, because they don't know a thing about it. After the lunch, if the account chairman is feeling good, he'll give the account to the agency chairman on the spot because he trusts him and 'he's our kind of person.' However, with so much more money at stake these days, this kind of pitch is going out of style. Only once did I ever run into a guy I knew when I was a kid in Brooklyn. We were pitching a radio station and this kid who used to hang around the same street corner as I did turned out to be the account executive of the radio station. It was the first time I ever had a common background with a potential account. We sat around talking about old times, you know, things like 'Hey, whatever happened to Baldy?' 'I don't know.' 'What happened to Louie Nuts?' 'Well Louie Nuts is doing three to five in Dannemora.' 'And how about Whacky?' 'Whacky?' 'Yeah, you remember, Whacky was the guy with the funny pointy head.' 'Oh, yeah, Whacky.' It turns out that out of the first twenty years of his life, Whacky spent ten in various prisons. I'm not very good on pitches that depend on schoolboy chums.

CHAPTER TWELVE

PROFILES IN WARM AND HUMANE COURAGE

'Presentations are like an opening night on Broadway. It's very big, it's the make-or-break moment for an agency, and there is a lot of very tough pressure on everyone. You've got thirty-six minutes and your audience is sitting there, and like who knows what's going to happen? Sometimes you barely get the presentation off the ground before disaster strikes . . .'

Good agencies refuse to work up a free presentation. The agency which is forced to work up a presentation is an agency that is in trouble. It's an agency that is desperate, insecure about showing the work they've already done. There was a soap commercial on the air and it featured a little girl running up to her mother with a slip which had just been washed in the soap, and the little girl says, 'Mommy, smell my slip.' Now if you're the agency that turned out that little job you really don't want to go showing it to prospective clients, do you? All right, so a possible client comes to you and says, 'We don't like what our present agency is doing for us creatively, what can you do?' Well, you're faced with the prospect of either showing the little girl smelling her slip or turning out something on spec. What is happening today in all of advertising is accounts are coming in to talk creative. The main source of dissatisfaction that accounts have is in the creative area.

When an agency has no smarts in an area like the creative area, they have to go to a pitch. So they come up with a campaign. They work as though they had the account. They go out and take pictures, they work up marketing plans, spend fortunes on shooting rough commercials. They spend thousands of dollars. They get photographers to work for them for reduced rates. They say, O.K., do this for half price now and you can sock one of my clients later when we come to you.' The current clients of the agency end up paying for presentations. If there is a scandal in the business, it's the money that clients are paying for work that they never see. A typical example: A large agency has a presentation to do. They write off a lot of it. They take the bills they get for the presentation and spread them throughout the other accounts in the agency. Let's say they get a $400 stat bill for the presentation. They'll dump that $400 on the twenty accounts that they have in the agency. So it's $20 an account, and what does the account know?

When they tell their art director to do something as cheaply as possible, the only thing the art director can say to the photographer is to do it for half price now with the promise that he can sock it on the next bill. Type bills: same thing happens. Sure, they get somebody to cut the type bill, but that type bill shows up later on in some other poor guy's bill. Instead of paying $25 for something, he winds up paying $29. He doesn't question it – what does the client know about the cost of setting type? – it's only a $4,00 difference. The type people aren't going to absorb the loss. Somebody has to pay for it, so the existing clients foot the bill. When an agency does a full-scale presentation, somebody has to pay for it – that's obvious. What isn't so obvious is that the current clients have to do the paying. How do you think a prospective client would feel if, during a pitch, he was told that this pitch came to him through the courtesy of the other clients at the agency? He'd think the way I would – swell, but what happens if I give you my business? Do I have to pay for pitches you're going to make in the future? Think of the time spent on pitches. The account executive, the art director, copywriters, media people, research people, all of these guys working on a new pitch. If they're spending their time thinking about new business, they're not thinking about their regular accounts. This is very unfair. It's unfair of an advertiser to ask for a campaign and it's very unfair of an agency to accept the offer to make a pitch with a full campaign.

I would say that most of the smaller and newer agencies won't touch a pitch if a campaign is asked for. The reason for this is partly pride and partly common sense. Smaller agencies work like hell – they've got fewer people per account than larger agencies do and they really don't have the time to start pulling people off regular accounts to prepare a campaign. We do what a lot of agencies do: a regular, standard, straight-up pitch. It runs exactly thirty-six minutes – no more, no less. We show what we've done in the past, we give a one-minute philosophy of our approach, we answer any questions the account might have, and that's that. If we don't get the account, we didn't deserve to get it. They know as much about us in those thirty-six minutes as they ever will know. We've got our pitch broken down to seven minutes of commercials. Then you show your print ads, explain a bit about the background of each ad, and that's that.

Presentations are like an opening night on Broadway. It's very big, it's the make-or-break moment for an agency, and there is a lot of very tough pressure on everyone. You've got thirty-six minutes and your audience is sitting there, and like who knows what's going to happen? Sometimes you barely get the presentation off the ground before disaster strikes. Ron Travisano and I made a pitch not long ago to a very nice guy named Jerry O'Reilly, who handled the Evening in Paris perfume business. We walked into the offices and they were the slickest offices I've seen in a long time. We gave our names to a receptionist and this guy comes down this great long hall. This guy is Mr. O'Reilly's assistant. He leads us to this great big room where we are to meet Mr. O'Reilly. I was carrying the regular ad case and Ron was carrying the projector, which is a big thing and must weigh sixty or seventy pounds. Mr. O'Reilly walks in and I extend my hand and say, 'Mr. O'Reilly, I'm Jerry Della Femina.' He shakes my hand and then Ron turns to him and says, 'Hi, I'm Ron Travisano.' What Ron didn't remember as he turned to O'Reilly was that he was carrying that projector. When he turned, so did the projector, and the thing caught O'Reilly right on the kneecap. The sound of the projector hitting his kneecap was a sound I used to hear when I was a kid going to watch the Dodgers at Ebbets Field. You would listen to the crack of the bat and you could tell from the sound when it was going to be a home run. Same sound from O'Reilly's knee. I had my eyes shut when I heard that sound, and I could have sworn that his knee was going to end up in the left-field stands. O'Reilly went down to the floor immediately.

Ron turned to me right at the crack of the bat and said, 'This is not going to be such a good presentation.' And like I flipped when he said that. We both went into hysterics. Tears were coming out of my eyes. The guy, he went down and he had a little trouble talking for a few minutes. Ron and I went into such hysterics that we couldn't move – we were useless for the rest of the presentation. O'Reilly was very nice about it, considering that he might have been crippled for life by the shot. I'm sorry to say we didn't get the account – which is not surprising – and the guy was nice enough not to sue us for bodily damage with intent to kill.

Just after we went into business for ourselves we had a chance to pitch an account over in Jersey – some outfit that made hair tonic. They wanted to see what we had done in the past and we decided to ship all of our previous ads out to Jersey ahead of time. Ron lives in Jersey and he said he would take the portfolio out there the day before, since it was on his way home. Ron sometimes dresses a little too much. This particular day he was wearing a bright-green sport jacket plus an electric-blue shirt, and to top that off he had on one of those flowered ties. He's got very swarthy skin and very weird hair and occasionally when you take a look at him he comes on a little strange. He gets out to Jersey with the portfolio and he tells the receptionist he's the executive vice-president of the agency and they show him to the office of Mr. Jones, the guy we're supposed to pitch. Jones comes to the door and Ron starts to say that he's from the agency but Jones takes one look at Ron and figures him for a Mercury Messenger or something. 'O.K., thanks, boy,' Jones says, and leaves poor Ron standing there. It was obvious that if Ron had a piece of paper in his hand Jones would have signed it and sent him on his way. Like Ron was destroyed for three days after that. It was the first time he had ever been mistaken for a messenger.

Sometimes presentations turn into disasters because you find out halfway through that you really shouldn't have been there in the first place. Years ago I worked for a short time at an agency called Ashe & Engelmore. One of the guys at the agency named Bob Hirshberg had met another guy at the bar of '21' and after two minutes of talk Bob figured that the guy was hinting that we should go out and make a very big presentation for the Loew's Hotel business in Puerto Rico. I don't know to this day how Bob got that impression, but he came back to the agency and said, 'This is it, we've got a real shot at this account.'

Well, we sat down and I get the bright idea that we've got to find out more about how travel agents react to the Americana Hotel. I got a little tape recorder with an attachment to the telephone and we started to call travel agents. I decided that I would tell them that I'm a guy going to Puerto Rico and could they recommend a hotel. If they don't recommend the Americana, then I would say, 'Hey, how about the Americana? Is that any good?' Then we'd take the tape and use it at the presentation.

I got a tapeload of reactions. Little did I know that things like this can blow a whole presentation. I figured the tape would immediately strike them that they needed an agency like us, one that thought ahead and really was interested enough to know the problems that they might be facing. At the first meeting I knew something was wrong when the guy whom Bob had met in the bar said, 'Bob, you didn't have to do anything like this.' Bob says, 'Well, we thought we would show you what our ideas on the . . .' And the guy said, 'Look, I thought this would just be a meeting where we would talk a little bit.' When you hear that phrase, duck. Also sitting in at the meeting was one of the Tisch brothers – I forgot which – but one of the owners of Loew's Hotels.

They're waiting for the presentation to start and I said, 'Gentlemen, I'd like you to hear this tape.' The tape goes on, you hear the telephone ringing, and my voice saying, 'Is this the Magic Carpet Travel Service?' 'Yeah.' 'My name is Jerry Dell and I'm looking for a place to stay when I go to Puerto Rico. I was wondering if you could tell me something about the place.' And the travel agent's voice comes on, 'Well, there are a lot of nice places in Puerto Rico.' One of the Loew's guys says, 'That's Hymie Smith.' They start whispering around the table, 'Hey that's Hymie, that's Hymie.'

I said, 'What place would you recommend?' Hymie says, 'Well, I would recommend . . .' and he recommended something other than the Americana. My voice comes on again. 'What about the Americana? I hear a lot about the Americana.' Hymie says, 'The Americana? It's too close to the airport. It hasn't got a swinging crowd. You're a young guy, right?'

The next voice I hear is one of the Loew's Hotel people who says, 'That prick! Stop the tape!' I stop the tape and the hotel guy tells a secretary to call in a guy named Sid, who evidently is in charge of travel-agent relations. Sid is a very fat guy and when he walks in he's very cordial and gives everybody a big smile and makes a big thing of shaking all hands. 'Sid,' says the hotel guy, 'when's the last time you spoke to Hymie Smith over at Magic Carpet Travel?' 'Hymie? I took Hymie to lunch just the other day.' 'Would you say that Hymie is your friend?' 'Oh, Hymie is one of our good friends.' 'Play the tape.' I replay the tape and Sid is perspiring a lot.

At this point I'm ready to go into the presentation. They couldn't care less. At this point they're so aggravated at Hymie over at Magic Carpet Travel that they don't know I'm in the room. 'Well,' I say, 'now I'd like to show you what we're going to do to combat this indifference to your hotel.' Nobody's listening. The Loew's guy is going on in this vein – 'You spend money, you take these guys to places I don't go to, and then they show you this? Those bastards have no loyalty.' Guys are walking around muttering, 'How could you spend money on those bastards?'

I try to butt in with 'I'd like to tell you how we're going to solve this marketing problem of yours ...' One hotel guy looked at me as if to say, 'What, are you still here? You caused all the trouble, you bum, now go away.' I said, 'Here's an ad we have featuring James Bond...' One guy says, 'Look. We got advertising, we got good advertising. We're not interested in a new agency. We're worried about the off season.'

Meanwhile we're trying to back out the door without getting hit. Now it's a case where you have to grab your equipment, and suddenly it feels like you have a lot more equipment than when you went in. You're plugging things and unplugging things and the tape recorder is falling on the floor and 'Bob, hold this,' 'I got it,' and they're still yelling at Sid. The whole thing was such a disaster that it probably was the greatest thing that ever happened to me in advertising because I learned one thing out of it: that was, never be afraid of a presentation. I mean, what could go worse? Worse is that they could physically attack you. That is the end. I've seen people who were uptight about presentations. A lot of people. Agency presidents who get very shook about presenting. And I always think back to that day with Loew's as Bob and I were walking out. I was trying to hold my head in my hands and keep the tape recorder under one arm.

On the street it was murder. A hot, hot day in July, and it must have been like 98 degrees out. When we got downstairs the heat hit us. Now usually whenever an agency finishes a presentation, no matter how bad it is, they usually say, 'Did you notice that guy over there on the end? He looked pretty impressed. The other two were yawning but . . .' They always try to find something to get them through the day. Nobody doesn't get an account. You always say, 'Gee, we got a good chance.' When Bob and I came down the elevator we were still looking back to see if they were chasing us. They were shoving us out the door saying things like 'Here, take this. This is the top to that thing you're carrying. You can snap it on later.'

So there we are, 98 degrees out, carrying all this equipment. I start to say something in the usual vein about the presentation and Bob looked at me and said, 'Shhh. Don't even talk about it.' We're lugging all of this equipment and of course no cabs. We had to walk back from Forty-third and Broadway to Madison Avenue at Thirty-eighth Street. It was like the Bataan Death March. We were sweating, we were dying, the heat was killing us. I felt like people were hitting me with bayonets to get me going.

We got back to the agency and Irwin Engelmore, the

president, a very sweet guy, takes a look at the two of us who are soaked through and says, 'How'd you do?' And for the first time in the history of advertising someone told the truth after a presentation. Bob said, 'We bombed.' Irwin said, 'Oh, were there things that they didn't like?'

Bob said, 'There was everything that they didn't like. We bombed.'

Now Irwin, who had spent quite a bit of money on this presentation, said, 'Well, do they want us to come back again?'

Bob said, 'I don't think they want us in that neighborhood any more. I don't think we can go around Broadway and Forty-second Street.'

Irwin said, 'Uh, is there somebody I can call?'

'I don't know,' he said. 'Call a priest, Irwin. Maybe he'll help.'

Once, also at Ashe & Engelmore, we were going to make a presentation to a fellow named Richard Meltzer, who was the president of Beauknit Mills, a very big textile company. We had come up with some kind of campaign to show them – I don't even remember what it was, it's not really important. The thing was we all had instructed Irwin before the presentation, 'Irwin, when you go out there, when you sit down with this guy, don't forget he's going to ask you some questions about what kind of advertising they need. This is new to him. Remember, it's *human* advertising. I want you to tell him it's human advertising.' I would do this to Irwin all the time, set him up, get him straight. 'You got it now? It's *human* advertising you're showing. If he says, 'What is it?' tell him it's warm and human.'

Irwin said, 'Yeah, yeah. It's warm and human.'

I said, 'Right, Irwin. It's warm and human, warm and

human, warm and human.' He said, 'Don't worry about it, Jerry. We're going to do well.'

Irwin gets to the presentation and he's sitting there with his right-hand man, a very bright guy named Lee Barnett. Irwin hands Meltzer the campaign and says, 'Mr. Meltzer, this is it. This is humane.' Barnett's muttering, 'No, no, no.' Irwin says, 'It's humane, Mr. Meltzer. This is humane advertising, warm and humane.' Barnett's whispering, 'It's human, it's human.' Irwin says, 'Yeah, human. It's humane, Mr. Meltzer.' Finally Barnett kicked Irwin under the table and said, '*Human!* Humane is kind to dogs, you schmuck!'

Irwin was a good man on presentations. He would always start off his presentation by saying, 'Do you have the courage to run our kind of advertising?' And the prospective client usually was confused because he couldn't figure out what kind of advertising he had to have the courage to run. This was Irwin's standard pitch. Most agency presidents have a standard pitch where they say, 'It takes courage to run our kind of advertising' or 'It doesn't take courage to run our kind of advertising.' Or 'We're marketers' or 'We're salesmen' or whatever they are on any given Thursday. Irwin's pitch always was the courage pitch. Running his ads was a sign of virility. It was wonderful, just wonderful.

Pitching with Shep Kurnit was just as much fun as it was with Irwin. Kurnit is a brilliant guy. He could be very good. We compete pretty hard against each other but I like the guy. He's got tremendous staying power. It's hard to keep up with him. He stays. He claws, he scratches, he fights, but he's there. He's not a pushover by any means. One of his funny traits is that when he talks to you he's got to touch you. When he makes a point, he touches you. The touching used to drive us crazy. One day Ron came out of his office and said, 'I solved the problem. Whenever he comes near me and starts to touch me, I start lighting matches.' Shep always used to back you in a corner. Ron said, 'It's easy. You stand there lighting matches and he never comes near you any more.'

One of Shep's little idiosyncrasies was that during a pitch he usually would find fault with the product they were pitching. As I said, he's very bright, and quite often during presentations he would take a look at the thing and automatically redesign it before your eyes. The problem was that you never knew when Shep was going to redesign the client's product and this led to a lot of tension at new-business meetings at Delehanty. You never knew when Shep was going to drop the bomb. Maybe the client has been in business for fifty years and maybe his father had started making these widgets or whatever. This guy has lived with these widgets for years, he wakes up widgets, he sleeps and dreams widgets. Shep would come in, take one look at the widget and say, 'You know what? If you took this handle off here, put the handle there, changed this, switched that, then you'd have a hell of a product.' It was great because it gave you a chance to become reacquainted with your shoes. You would look at them and after a while Shep would be finished with redesigning the product.

The great thing about Shep is that he would drop a bomb on you in the unlikeliest places. Once we had to attend a Group W (Westinghouse) affiliates' convention in Florida. Shep had given a little speech the day before, and on this day we were sitting around the pool having lunch: Shep, Marvin Davis (a vice-president of Delehanty), me, and the lady in charge of continuity for the Group W stations. She was a very prim and proper lady because if you're in charge of continuity you've got to be at least a virgin, if not better. We're sitting there eating and I'm waiting for the bomb to fall. We know it's going to happen, so Marvin and I are trying to pick easy subjects to talk about. Marvin was picking good subjects like the weather, I was picking good subjects like baseball, we both were picking very good. The directress of continuity must have thought we were crazy, but little did she know! The minute he zapped in that this woman is in charge of continuity, he had to do continuity stories. He started off by saying, 'I have a client who is a great guy, but I once had a problem selling him an ad for Talon Zippers that showed the Statue of Liberty with a zipper down her back.' He goes into the whole story about how he has to create ads all day long on zippers, and I kind of looked over at Marvin for a second and he had a sandwich up to his mouth and his eyes rolled to the back of his head. We both knew something bad was going to happen but we weren't quite sure what. I said to myself, 'He's not going to tell the old Statue of Liberty story – he's not going to do that.'

Sure enough. He says, 'We had this ad with the Statue of Liberty and I knew how the client would react to the Statue having her zipper in the back open. He could say it's unpatriotic – but I remembered something I once saw on Forty-second Street.'

I said to myself, 'Oh, oh, here's where he tells the story about how he picked up a Statue of Liberty with a thermometer in its backside in some souvenir store on Forty-second Street. *Oh, Shep, please don't talk about the thermometer being in the backside.*'

Shep came through, all right. He did not say the Statue of Liberty had the thermometer in its backside. He said, 'So when I took the client this Statue of Liberty with a thermometer shoved up its ass I told him if they can shove a thermometer up the ass of the Statue of Liberty, you can take a zipper down in the back.' Like it was the first time someone really said a prayer after a meal. Everybody had their heads down at their plates, reading their parsley.

You can't underestimate Shep. One day he was flying back to New York from I don't know where and he happened to be sitting next to the advertising manager in charge of Singer Sewing Machines of Peru. Shep talked to him during the plane ride and the guy got to like Shep and he gave Shep the account. It was one of the most beautiful accounts in the history of advertising. We were selling sewing machines to Indians who couldn't run them because they had no place to plug them in. Shep went out and researched things and we found that the best form of media in Peru was to put a sign on a boat that floats down the Amazon River – or whatever river flows through Peru.

Singer of Peru was a great experience. I once wrote an ad that said, 'The machine you buy your mother on Mother's Day will last until Father's Day.' It went to the client off in Peru and it came back with the note, 'We have no Father's Day in Peru.' We had a girl in our office who was a student from Colombia and was some kind of an Indian and she knew the kind of Spanish that they spoke in Peru – at least she said she did – and she would translate everything we did and then we would send it down to Peru.

A crazy account. We had an American who understood the language to shoot commercials for us, so we wrote this one commercial which showed a young man and a young woman walking into the local Singer Sewing Center. Well, our man in Peru gets the storyboard for the commercial and he didn't know where to go to hire the models for the shooting. So this guy did what he thought was a logical thing. He went to a local movie studio and hired a couple of young out-of-work actors. The next day as our guy got ready to go out to shoot the commercial, he happened to glance at the local newspaper. There, staring back at him, was the face of his male model on page 1, and across his chest was a string of numbers. It turned out that the actor had just been picked up by the local police when he had attempted to hold up the National Bank of Lima. Our cameraman called us up in New York and informed us that the commercial we were waiting for would have to be held up for three to five years.

I had written a nice little commercial which showed a bullfighter sitting in the middle of a ring, sewing himself a cape. They let the bull out and the bullfighter starts sewing like a son of a bitch. Then the commercial cuts to the bull, back to the bullfighter, back to the bull, until the last moment when he finished the cape just in time to give the bull a pass and save his neck. The way it was shot, the opening scene showed the bullfighter wearing a black suit and in the next shot he was wearing a white suit, and in the third shot he had on a suit with a lot of crazy decorations on it. They just found some stock film and put it in wherever they could.

You wonder why Peru is mad at us. We were selling them machines and the poor Indians were buying machines without power. On time, yet. We got a letter from a guy who was trying to make a collection from a couple of Indians who had bought a sewing machine. They were stuck away on a mountain someplace and the collection guy spent four hours going through swamps, jungles and who knows what else trying to reach them. He was able to see them but he could not get to them. He could never reach them and he couldn't understand how they ever got down off their perch to get the sewing machine and put it on the back of their donkey and go back up the mountain.

The Peru guy used to show up in New York every so often and Shep spent hours trying to teach the guy media. The Peru guy says, 'You have to go in this magazine, *El Commandore*.' Shep says, 'What about this other magazine, *El Fig*?' (You had a choice of two magazines in your Peru marketing plan.) The Peru guy says, '*El Fig* is no good because it's never on the newsstands. You can't advertise in it.' Shep says, 'Why isn't it on the stands?' He's figuring maybe they're having union trouble with *El Fig* down in Peru. The local tells Shep, 'The minute *El Fig* comes out it disappears from the stands. But *El Commandore*, it's always around on the stands.' Shep says, 'Do you understand that people are buying *El Fig* and not buying *El Commandore* and that's why *El Fig* is never around and *El Commandore* is?' The Peru guy said, 'Oh.' We ran ads, we ran commercials, and we made a lot of bread. If you got the Indian to make the down payment, you were breaking even. The rest of the stuff was gravy.

The best presentation I ever took part in also was at Delehanty. We were getting ready for a presentation to Chemway, Inc., which makes Pretty Feet. Usually, the night before any presentation Shep would come in and suddenly decide that everything was wrong and we were not going to get the account. True to form, he came in the night before the Chemway pitch and said our stuff was garbage and we wouldn't get the account. Well, we had a terrible fight. Shep and I were always having terrible fights – but this one was worse. Marvin Davis, who also would be in on the pitch, said something about one of the ads and I went berserk. I had been working very hard and I just flipped. I climbed over a table after Marvin. People had to pull us apart because it was turning into a real brawl.

I was so uptight about what had just happened that I went out drinking for the whole night. It was a very wild night and I woke up at seven o'clock in the morning in a strange place not knowing what to do for clothing because my clothes were a shambles. I knew that I had to make a presentation and my shirt looked as if somebody had thrown up on it – maybe it was me. I had to find a shirt, if nothing else. The presentation was scheduled for nine o'clock. No store is open at 8:30. I had a car and I couldn't remember where I had parked it. So I left the car wherever it was and jumped into a cab and told the guy to take me down to the West Side waterfront. Down there the Army-Navy surplus stores are open all night. I bought a denim shirt and a solid blue tie and figured it wouldn't look too bad. I was still hung over, terribly so, and I took the cab back to the office to make the presentation.

During a presentation the top-ranking officer from the agency starts the pitch and then everybody around the table says his piece, including the creative department. And now it comes time for me to do my speech and somebody had given me a cup of coffee. The alcohol must have been condensed in my body, because the minute I got the coffee down I was drunk again. But I got up and made the best presentation I've ever made in my life. It wasn't that I thought I was good; people came up to me at the end of the presentation and said, 'I've seen you at a presentation before but I've never seen you so buttoned up.' Well, the buttoned-up part was that I was afraid to open my mouth and really talk because I figured if I did open up my mouth I would throw up. So I talked very quietly. Afterward everyone said, 'Usually you get very excited. This was so nice. You didn't move, you didn't jump around. This was just the way to present to these people.' Little did they know that if I had jumped around my head would have fallen on the table.

They gave us the account on the spot. I ordered champagne for everybody but I wouldn't serve any to Shep or Marvin. We got drunk the same day. It was like one twenty-four-hour binge, the whole place just went crazy.

Once, at Delehanty, we made a terrific presentation and the president of the company we were pitching fell asleep when the lights went out during the showing of the commercials. Shep was very good that day, and Marvin Davis was very good, too. I was sitting next to the president and he just didn't like the whole group. He was getting very tight and very fidgety. When a presentation is packaged, as the Delehanty presentation was, it's very hard to stop. It's like when you stop a door-to-door salesman in the middle of his pitch, he'll get so confused that he'll start the whole pitch over again. Shep's presentation couldn't be cut at the right time or speeded up. The presentation went on, deadly.

The lights went out for the reel of commercials. I'm watching this old guy. The lights went out, he went out. He had his head resting on his chest and if you looked at him in the dark, you would imagine that he was thinking very hard. He must have had a clock in him or maybe his advertising manager was bumping him but all of a sudden toward the next to the last commercial on the reel he woke up. The last commercial went off and he woke up completely. And he's one of these guys who when he just wakes up he's not a nice guy. He woke up a tiger and started taking people apart. 'And you? What do you do?' he said to a girl. 'What qualifies you to be on my account?' The girl was very nervous. 'Well, uh, you see . . .' 'Are you on my account,' he says, 'or are you one of these people that they brought in to impress me?' 'No, no,' the girl said, 'I'm a fashion coordinator.' 'What do I need with a fashion coordinator?' he said. It went on like that. Finally, he got to Kurnit. 'Mr. Kurnit, why is your agency, of all the agencies I've seen – why is your agency qualified to handle my account?' This is a very tough question. 'Well,' said Shep, 'one of the reasons that I'm qualified is because our agency has been looking for this type of account for many years . . .' 'I know you're looking for my account. I want to know if you can handle it now.' The problem was he was just not a nice guy when he woke up. He took them apart.

At Fuller & Smith & Ross, one of the problems we had when we made a pitch was that one of the account supervisors – a klutz named Harry – was so inept he would blow everything almost right from the start. He claimed to have worked on almost every great campaign that ever came out of J. Walter Thompson, which was where he was at before he conned his way into Fuller & Smith. 'Pan Am, oh yeah. I remember when we were doing Pan Am.' He may have been in the building when they were working on the Pan Am account. He was fantastically uncoordinated. He would sit there with his pipe and talk, and invariably the phone would ring. He would reach for the phone and knock the pipe out of his mouth. Every time. Once, right before a meeting, Mike Lawlor saw him in the men's room brushing his pants off. Harry said, 'Got to go to a new-business meeting. Spilled some powder on my pants.' He finally got the pants perfectly clean and said, 'O.K., now I can go into the meeting.' He walked into the meeting with his fly open. He set the indoor record for showing up at meetings with his fly open.

They finally ran this guy out of New York but he survived. He went to Rome, billing himself as the great white hope of New York. They just booted him out of Rome but he's got at least nine other countries to go. The guy has Germany; he hasn't touched France yet. He's got plenty of places in Europe. When they catch on to him in Europe he can come back here to some off-the-wall place like Topeka. 'Here I am,' he'll say. 'I ran an agency in Rome for a while but now I'm ready to come back to Topeka because I've got this little lung condition and I wanted some of that fresh air of Topeka and I think I'm going to really make your agency.' Topeka, they fall for it.

Guys get nervous before presentations, very uptight. Some guys throw up before presentations. There are some agency presidents who are basically shy, and when they present, they are being called on to do things that they never really wanted to do. In what other business does the president of the company go out and solicit the business? Salesmen get business. If your salesmen aren't getting the business, then you call in the sales manager and straighten him out. If a guy wants to go and be handled by a law firm, the partners don't show up and tell him what their law firm is going to do for him and what clients they've kept out of jail in the past. But in advertising you don't get an account without the client getting to see the president of the agency.

It's just as tough on the other side. The client has to pick an agency, and let's say that the field has been narrowed down to four finalists. Here he's about to commit $3 million or $4 million to a bunch of guys and he has to evaluate them in an hour or so. And you know what? All four of them start to look alike after a while, and nowadays they say the same thing.

Cliché number one is: We're the most creative agency in New York City.

They'll even give you a tour of their creative department. Then the prospective client sees guys in their offices who have hair jumping out of their heads as if they had stuck their tongue in an electric socket. 'That guy over there, we have to keep him strapped in. You know, he goes berserk from time to time. But wow, what an art director!' They'll point to a copywriter: 'Very good. You'll never have to deal with him. We don't deal with him ourselves except when it's feeding time.' Bates was always very big at showing clients the creative department. Let's face it, my section *was* crazy, guys yelling, secretaries screaming. It looked strange as hell. Delehanty, which has some genuine crazy people, downplays the talk about them. They talk about their advertising. It's like an arms race, this creative stuff. Our nuts are nuttier than anyone else's. We have more madmen per square inch than any other agency. Therefore we are creative. I think any client who falls for that is really pretty naïve, but some still do.

Cliché number two is: We've got some of the great success stories in the business.

Everybody has a success story. If you go by presentations, there has never been a product that failed in American history. Everybody succeeds. We took such and such, which had a losing share of the market, and now they're number one. We took this thing here which was a new product and now it leads the field.

After a while the agency guys all start to run together. They all are very sharp, very charming. The guys are going to be charming, they're going to be witty, they're going to be bright, they're going to stare at the client, at the tip of the guy's nose, and appear to be staring deeply into his eyes. They're going to do all the things that they learned about over the years. They're going to be so good at it that they all look alike.

The only thing that the guy can really depend on is the work. If I were a client, I would not even want to see any agency people until I was just about to make my decision. Then, if they didn't turn out to be gorillas, I would give them the business. I've worked at five different agencies and I've never seen anything said at a presentation that is any different from what we say now. We're all in the same bag. We all say the same things.

Oh, sure, some guys pose. They say, 'I don't know if I can take your account.' Very funny. Deep down they're saying, 'If you give it to me, I'll be sure to figure out a way to take it.' But basically we're all the same. We're all bright, we're all witty, we're all smart, we all know the client's problems, we all know how to solve them. It's a very tough sell, but it's a very tough buy, too. It's very tough for a client to buy an agency. He's always going to wonder if he made the wrong decision. He's always going to wonder if maybe those other guys he let go out the door had a little more magic. He's got to go on past record – that's the only thing. And that's where we live or die as an agency. That's all we have. I don't play golf. Ron plays golf but he gets very hostile on the golf course, so we can't go looking for new business on the course. I've never had a client to dinner at my home. Neither has Ron. You don't need us for any of the other things. Join a friendship club for that kind of stuff. We'll take a client to dinner – to discuss business.

Not long ago we made a pitch and we were competing with Doyle, Dane and Wells, Rich, and Jack Tinker. Three very strong agencies. I didn't figure we would get the business but I thought it was nice to be in such company. Suddenly it's reported in the papers that none of the four agencies got the account – it went to a very, very bad agency. One of those places where they strive for mediocrity and miss. Now this bad agency did not present – they were nowhere. They certainly couldn't get the account on the basis of their past work. Somewhere along the line, somebody made a hit, somebody scored. I figure they got the account through their bank. This bad agency found out who the client's bank was and worked a deal. It's so sad, because this client really needed a good agency to bail them out of their problems. Doyle, Dane would have been terrific for them, or Wells, Rich, or even us, but the outfit they gave the account to will run them into the ground. The sales will continue to drop and they will wonder why they can't move their product out.

Sometimes agency presidents are pretty casual guys themselves – forget about the writers and art directors. Charlie Goldschmidt is that kind of president – not uptight at all. Charlie has a thing about fire engines, or maybe it's fires. He would chase fire engines down the block. We might be having a presentation and Charlie would be sitting there quietly when, whammo, he'd hear a siren outside. He would jump up, run out the door, and you wouldn't see him for an hour or so. Some days I would be sitting with him alone and if he heard an engine he'd open the window. If it looked like the fire was close enough, he'd go out and see it. He was a big man for fires. One day in the middle of a very important meeting, Danny Karsch and a few other people were discussing things with a prospective client when he heard fire engines. The door to the office slams open, Charlie comes busting through. He walked right through the offices not saying a word to anyone, opened the window to check how close the fire was, shut the window, walked out, and shut the door. Not one single word during all this. Everybody is looking at one another, and finally Danny said, 'I think that people who like fires really don't like people.'

Packaged presentations are put together like Broadway shows. There are word cues and the whole thing. In our presentation, I might be talking and I'll say, 'And on the subject of marketing . . .' and Tully Plesser of the Cambridge Marketing group, who occasionally does a research study for us, will say, 'On the subject of marketing, I would say that we can offer you the following . . .' At the end of the marketing piece Tully might say, 'And of course marketing is only as good as media.' Then we punch the media director who wakes up and says, '*Life* magazine, four-color, full page.' Some agencies have this thing down to such a science that they don't even need word cues; they look at one another.

Not long ago we pitched to a very big food company in Dallas. There was a lot of money at stake and we were very nervous – when you're talking about millions of dollars you can't help but be nervous. We left New York on a Thursday for a Friday-morning pitch. We rent a car at the Dallas airport and drive into town and check into the hotel. We know we're in a foreign country when a local takes a look at Ron, who happens to be dressed very quietly, and says, 'Hey, boy, why don't you get a haircut?' Ron is very tense and says, 'Up yours, Reb.' We have dinner that night at the local top restaurant, where the big dish is fried steak with enchiladas on the side.

The next morning, grits. Ron, who sweats a lot, is really doing a job. We pile into the rented car and start looking for the main office. The company we're pitching to is enormous but we couldn't find it. You stop the car at a corner and ask somebody where the main headquarters are and of course you can't understand what the guy says. He's talking a different language. We felt like tourists in a foreign country. We started the car again and Ron says, 'What did he say?' 'I don't know, I didn't understand him.' We keep driving through this maze in the hope that we'll find an American we can talk to. Finally we get to one guy who says something like the building we're looking for is two blocks down, turn to the right.

Sure enough, general headquarters. Last-minute nerves. 'Don't forget we're billing fifteen million.' 'Fifteen? I thought it was eighteen.' 'How many people we got working for us now?' 'I don't know, I haven't counted lately.' You're trying to get all your facts straight.

A guy from the company comes out and he's very friendly and personable: 'Hi, I'm Eddie Jones, come on in.' Immediately four guys try to go through the door at the same time. It always happens, and the door is only built to hold maybe half of a guy. There is always a bumping of bodies on the way in to a presentation. I am very nervous, picking up and putting down the portfolio. It is like playing shortstop at Yankee Stadium when you know that it's going to be O.K. if you ever get a ball hit in your direction. If somebody would ask you, 'What are you guys billing?' things would be all right. Nobody's doing that. All they're trying to be is friendly. They get you into a real Texas-sized conference room and you pray that there will be at least one guy there you will be able to understand. You start listening to the introductions and the hellos, and on a hello from one guy Ron leaned into my ear and said, 'New York!' Fantastic. One cat we could understand. He was from New York and it was a great feeling that we weren't alone in this foreign country.

We still have to pick the man who has got the clout in the room. There is always one guy in a room who is going to say yes or no. Finding this guy is a job all by itself. There can be real problems in searching out this guy. A guy I know once came into a meeting late. He sat down, looked at his papers, and when it was his time to go on he's looking right down the line at each guy to find the one he's going to zero in on. He spots one guy who looks like he's important and very inquisitive and says to himself, 'This is it.' He stared him straight in the eye all the way through the pitch, never taking his eye off him. He threw out the rest of the people, so help me, and sold and sold and sold. He forgot the whole room. When it was over he was convinced that he had done a terrific job. Then they told him he had been pitching to a new guy who had just come to work at his agency – an assistant media director. Obviously the new guy was too terrified to say, 'Hey, I'm on your team.'

There may be six people in the room and there's going to be discussion, but when it's all over one guy's going to say, 'I think we should go this way.' He might not even say that. He might say, 'The president, I think, will agree that we should go this way.' This is the guy you want to find.

You start off ad libbing and you have no idea whom you're talking to. They want to know where we ate the night before and when we tell them they say, 'Great place, great steak.' I keep thinking of the enchiladas. They're uncomfortable because they know you're nervous as hell. You start off by saying, 'I want to thank you all for allowing us to come out here and make this presentation.'

The top gunner, the big guy, is at this meeting. Which is not good. My feeling about top gunners is when they're at a meeting their troops feel they've got to perform for the top gunner. I like to go with plateaus.

The group we're pitching to, they're all big gunners. You could see it when the introductions started: 'Vice-President in charge of international operations'; 'Vice-President in charge of marketing'; 'Director of marketing and advertising.'

I start up again by thanking everyone. I give a little of my background and then we go around the table, and each of us gives background on himself. One of our account executives, Jim Travis, tells who he is. Ron tells them who he is – he's still nervous but he gets through it fine. Now we're back to what to do next. I still don't think it's time to show the work; neither does Ron, because the way we work Ron hands me the ads as I show them and he's not moving for the pile. I'm not even looking at him because I don't want to show, either. We started looking at each other around 8:30 a.m. and now it's about ten after nine. It's still not the right time and then one of the gunners asks me about a column I wrote in *Marketing/Communications*. I talk about the column and everybody laughs – I was attacking the Federal Government and guys in the food business live in fear of the Food and Drug Administration.

All of a sudden, now it's O.K. to show the work. We're very close to them and now the pitch becomes almost automatic. I start to look over at Ron but I don't have to because he's reaching to pick up the first sample of work. First I go into a disclaimer, telling them that some of the work they're going to see was done at three different agencies.

The first ad we show is the Peanuts ad for Talon Zippers. We do it because it gives the group a chance to laugh right off the bat. I tell them that I don't know whether the ad ever sold a zipper or not, but it was a good ad psychologically for all the clothing manufacturers who were looking at the ad to know about Talon. So you've opened the meeting and the feeling is warm and friendly; now you've got to hit them with something hard, so we show the Pretty Feet ad – the one that says, 'What's the Ugliest Part of Your Body?' A very good reaction on this one. They look impressed so I detour into drug advertising. Then, all of a sudden, there's a long discussion about Pretty Feet.

Plesser is there watching and waiting. The very second this guy asks me a question and I answer it, I know I haven't answered it right down the line. One second later the next voice I hear is Plesser's saying, 'And another side of it is . . .' Plesser adds a little more weight; he makes my answer palatable.

Corum Watches comes on next and before you know it the lights are out and the commercial reel is on. We open with the commercial for Ozone, a men's hairspray, which we did at Bates using Yogi Berra. Whenever that commercial is shown at a presentation, somebody's voice comes out of the dark saying, 'Look at the face on this guy.' The next commercial is one our own agency did for *The New York Knickerbocker*, a newspaper that began after the *World-Journal Tribune* folded. It folded pretty quickly itself. As it starts to play I always say, 'That commercial cost six thousand dollars to produce. These days you can't even get a baby picture of your kid for six thousand.' They all pick up. Now they're looking to see what we got for our six grand – which is something they toss away every hour. A Royal Globe Insurance commercial is next. In the final scene of this one a driver out of control is coming straight out of the screen at the viewer in a very dramatic night shot. Ron quietly gets up during this commercial and walks over to the projector. He looks as though he's fiddling with the focus, but what he really is doing is turning the sound of the commercial up full blast. The sound of the commercial fills the room just as the car is about to crash. As the commercial finishes, Ron turns down the sound and sits down again. This works very well and the guy next to me says, 'Wow!'

We close the reel with a commercial we did for the National Hemophilia Foundation, which features a bleeder bleeding on camera. On come the lights and then I go into the agency philosophy. Because this is a company with problems with the Government, I tell them about Miss Cheng and Feminique. They're nodding their heads, saying, 'Yeah. Thank God somebody else is being persecuted.' One old conservative guy at the meeting is saying, 'You mean you can talk about a woman's private parts and they won't let us say what we want to say about food?' He's very angry and as far as he's concerned he's got to go out and lynch a couple of Mexicans to feel better.

Then I talk about our billing – all of us had finally agreed on a figure which was reasonably accurate. Then I mention that we have had assignments from R.J. Reynolds and Quaker Oats. I repeat it three times because somebody might have thought it was the Quakertown Oats Company, which makes horse food. 'Yes, Quaker Oats called us and said, "We've decided to give you an assignment." Just to make sure, I throw in, 'Lovely people over at Quaker Oats.' If I could have, I would have asked them if they had their Quaker Oats for breakfast this morning. What I'm doing with Quaker Oats is establishing that although that company is bigger than our prospective client, *they* think we're respectable.

I talk about the American Broadcasting Company next. They all love the word 'American' in Dallas and they seem to have heard of ABC. Great second name to mention. From ABC I move to Cinzano Vermouth. I look over at the older guy. He looks as if he's thinking that we're in bed with all the Italians. 'That client also has Moët Champagne,' I add. He doesn't like the French either, right? So we go into Blue Nun wine – I almost get a smile out of him with Blue Nun wine. We've also done some special projects for a large account that they've heard of. All of a sudden little looks around the table. 'Look,' I say, 'they're very happy with their agency but it's practically the same situation where you called me and said you're not unhappy with your agency, either.' I talk about Corum Watches. Who knows from Corum Watches? 'Part of the Piaget Company.' Nobody stirs. 'Part of the North American Watch Company.' The old guy hears American and starts to nod.

Suddenly one guy asks, 'What do you think of Ted Bates?' I don't think much of Ted Bates in or out of a presentation so I start blasting Bates. They keep talking. The big question they bring up is, 'What happens if Della Femina gets run over by a truck?' They're worried about the fact that we appear to be a one-man operation. We have to convince them that they're wrong. We end up by leaving them with the impression that I was already dead at this meeting and stuffed just to make the presentation look nice.

We tell them that we've just moved into a new set of offices. We finish our pitch and that's that. We made plans for them to visit us in New York, which they want to do. Dates are set up, which is good. The only thing different we'll do is to take our art director, Bob Giraldi, and go get him a haircut and maybe dress him like an American. Otherwise nothing will change.

A few weeks later they did come up to see us. We went through the pitch again and walked them through the offices. We even had gotten Bob to wear some normal clothes for the occasion. We have a good shot at the business, too. Lots of handshaking and congratulations. The last thing one of their guys said as he left our offices was, 'Boy, you creative agencies sure have some strange types around. Like that art director of yours.'

CHAPTER THIRTEEN
THE MOST FUN YOU CAN HAVE WITH YOUR CLOTHES ON

Date Due Receipt

05/03/2017

Items checked out to

Migliore, Marylou

TITLE From those wonderful folks

BARCODE 31325004350124

DUE 05-31-17 00:00AM

DUE
BARCODE
TITLE

MA00:00 71:31 80

31320043802 54

From those wonderful folks

Michole Marion

Items checked out to

08/03/2017

Date Due Receipt

'New agencies always start at lunchtime. Everybody goes to lunch and everybody bitches at lunch. "Those sons of bitches, they don't appreciate what I've done for them. Why, in the last year I've picked up two millions' worth of billing myself." All of a sudden, "Imagine that. Two million dollars. That means three hundred thousand dollars to the agency and all I'm making from them is a lousy forty thousand a year. They're making three hundred thousand and paying me forty thousand. I'd really like to start a place." The other guy says, "You know, we've worked together for a lot of years. I haven't got any money but I've got a friend who's got all the money and he's got a connection. Let's go into business…" '

I am very poor on dates and it is a good thing I'm in the advertising business where they don't worry too much about how accurate résumés are. I was born in 1936 and in July I will be thirty-four years old. I got married when I was twenty years old but I really have been married all my life. I graduated from Lafayette High School in Brooklyn in 1954 and I went to night school at Brooklyn College for one year. That's it with regard to education. My first job was as a messenger boy for *The New York Times* and I really didn't do anything much beyond that from 1945 to 1961. In 1961 I finally got a job with a real advertising agency, Daniel & Charles.

I started with Danny and Charlie as a copywriter at $100 a week, and when I left in 1963 to go to Fuller & Smith & Ross I was making $18,000 a year. I didn't last too long at Fuller & Smith – no more than nine months or so – and the next place I worked, which was Ashe & Engelmore, was an even shorter time. In 1964 I went to work for Shep Kurnit at Delehanty, Kurnit & Geller and I lasted there a couple of years. From Delehanty I moved over to Ted Bates in 1966, making $50,000 a year plus all the grief they could give you. We started our own agency in September of 1967 after Ron went out and practically raised $80,000 all by himself. I knew very few people with $800, much less $80,000. This September we will celebrate our third anniversary in business and of course we will have a big party. I really don't know what we're billing, but it must be someplace around $20 million a year, which is not bad at all. We've got fifty-three people working for us and we're paying some of these people $40,000 or so a year, which is not too bad, either. We have never been fired by one of our accounts. We resigned a couple of small ones because of some trouble with them, and one account, *The Knickerbocker,* just disappeared. We have a company car, a Lincoln, and one weekend last summer I drove out in it with my family to Montauk for the weekend. I locked the keys to the car in the trunk just as we were about to come back, so there are still strange things that happen now and then.

Last summer, one of our clients mailed us a check for $400,000, which was to cover a lot of television buying, and Ron and I took a look at that check and started to giggle like kids. It is a very weird feeling to hold a check in your hand for that amount of money and not think about skipping town to Brazil. When we go to the Coast to shoot a commercial they are very nice to us at the Beverly Hills Hotel, and it's great to sit at the pool and get paged. Our banker is nice to us, too, and we even have a line of credit. Guys call us up and try to hustle us to go public, which I hope we will never do. We have terrific offices at 625 Madison Avenue, a full floor, and the day we moved into the place we ran out of space. I work crazy hours and not long ago I spent three days and nights trying to control an AC-DC actor who was starring in one of our commercials. This guy tried first to make it with every girl on the set and after he went through the chicks, he then started on the shooting crew.

We have come a long way in three years, baby, to steal one of Leo Burnett's lines. The year we went into business, about 140 agencies also started up. There are now ten of those new agencies left. The problem with all of these new agencies is that most of them are started by creative guys who really aren't business-oriented. And they start agencies for the wrong reasons. A guy gets fired and he decides to start an agency. Guys don't plan their agencies. They don't plan their growth and they wind up in trouble.

A friend of mine just opened an agency and he said, 'Gee, I don't know if I should work out of my house or if I should work out of a hotel.' I said, 'You'd better work out of a hotel. At least if you have a prospective client call you he won't get your mother on the phone.' He said, 'Yeah, I guess you're right.' I read in the paper the other day that he just started in a hotel – a hotel I'd never heard of. I thought I'd heard of every hotel in New York but I think this one is one of the Lyons hotels down in the Bowery. I don't know where he found it but he's in business. He'll fold.

New agencies always start at lunchtime. Everybody goes to lunch and everybody bitches at lunch. 'Those sons of bitches, they don't appreciate what I've done for them. Why, in the last year I've picked up two millions' worth of billing myself.' All of a sudden, 'Imagine that. Two million dollars. That means three hundred thousand dollars to the agency and all I'm making from them is a lousy forty thousand a year. They're making three hundred thousand and paying me forty thousand. I'd really like to start a place.' The other guy says, 'You know, we've worked together for a lot of years. I haven't got any money but I've got a friend who's got all the money and he's got a connection. Let's go into business.'

So the three of them get together, find an Uncle Sam hotel and go into business. The friend with the connection doesn't pan out; he can't raise the bread. The account executive who's got some kind of promise that he can have an account when he opens suddenly finds that he doesn't have any business. The man who tells you he's going to give you business doesn't give it to you and all of a sudden you can't get him on the phone.

It was very tough for us in the beginning. There were the four founding partners: Ron, myself, Frank Seibke, an art director, and Ned Tolmach, a copywriter, all of us from Bates. And two girls – Barbara Kalish and a kid named Sandy Levy. We were at 635 Madison Avenue then and we had too much space. Just the six of us rattling around in these big offices. We were sitting around making presentations, hoping against hope that the guys would invite us to see them at their offices instead of ours. We got a little business but after three months we were in deep trouble. It was December and one day Ned and Frank came in and said they were leaving. It was just too tough. That day, the day they left, was very bad. It was about four o'clock in the afternoon and we figured we had $11,000 left in the bank after three months. There was furniture and rent, salaries for us and nothing but money going out. The lawyer got $5,000 for setting us up and the accountant took a fee too. You're talking about $2,000 going out every week with nothing coming in and we were sitting there and we realized that we had less than $11,000 left. We figured that if we quit paying ourselves and stretched it as far and as wide as we could, we might be able to last until March. Here we were on December 8th, I think it was, and it dawned on me that it was like the worst day of all time.

We had a lot of guys saying to us, 'Well, you know, we were considering you but now that Frank and Ned have left, well . . .' We had this date staring at us, March 1, the doors close and the sheriff comes in and takes the furniture out. We would have continued to try, but can you imagine trying to pitch an account without having an office – without having at least a girl answering the phone? If Sandy was out sick and Barbara was out doing something, a potential client would call Jerry Della Femina & Partners and get a guy answering. It was so frustrating because you know that all you need is time and you realize by the end of February you're out of business.

Then I remembered something. One of my heroes, really, is Mike Todd. The great Mike Todd story is that once he had a show running at the Winter Garden in 1944 and it was about to close. It was some wartime thing with Gypsy Rose Lee in it and it was in terrible shape. Todd didn't have any money and he didn't know what to do. He needed at least six months to get his money back and he can't buy a customer for love or money. So he threw out the guy he had at the box office and hired a lady who had arthritis very bad. She could move her hands, but very slowly.

Somebody would come up to the box office to buy a ticket and it would take her maybe ten minutes to make change. The day he hired her he was in business. She took so long that she built a line. Every time three people tried to buy a ticket the line grew. Pretty soon they had lines all around the Winter Garden. People would see the lines and ask, 'What show is going on here?' It was fantastic, and then Walter Winchell wrote an item in his column to the effect that 'They're standing around the corner to get into the Winter Garden.' Which was true, they were. The only trouble was the lady couldn't make change fast enough. The show suddenly turned into a big hit, ran for eight more months, and Todd got his money out.

What I did that bad day in December was decide that we needed something like Todd did. Ron said, 'What are we going to do?' I said, 'We're going to have a party.' Ron said, 'Are you crazy?' 'No,' I said. 'We're going to have the biggest Christmas party on Madison Avenue. We're going to invite every potential client we know. We are going to load this place up so with people that we will have to get two bartenders. We're going to have a photographer come down from *ANNY* and *Ad Age* to cover it. We are going to look so affluent that it's going to hurt.'

We must have sent out a thousand invitations. The place was so packed you couldn't move. We had the press, we had friends, we had enemies, we had potential new business, we had everybody. The party cost us like $3,000 and we knew that if this didn't work we were really sunk. But we pulled it off. People kept coming up to me that night saying, 'You know, I heard that things weren't going along so good but boy, you've got a place here, haven't you?' And we said, 'Things are going great, man.' Barbara was watching the bartender very carefully and I kept thinking we might end up eating the leftover food ourselves. We had guys who had come in from New Jersey for the party. We had all of our ads hanging up. You could hear it beginning to start. One guy would say, 'What are you here for?' And the other guy, 'Oh, I've been interested in this agency for quite a while and we're considering them.' All of us were almost high at the party and we didn't touch a drop of booze. My job was to walk around radiating confidence, you know, 'Hi, how's everything with you, how's your account doing?'

And the next day we got a call from an insurance company, the guy decided he's going to give us his business. The Moxie Company called the day after that and there we were: in business. The pictures started appearing in the trade papers and people around town were talking about Della Femina's Christmas party. It was a big thing and it made us. People began calling us, saying, 'You know, you people must be doing all right after all.' The party was the turning point for us. If we hadn't thrown the party and just tried to stretch the money out, we would have died. Guys would have been too suspicious. We had too many empty walls to convince anyone we were a going concern. Part of this business – a big part of it – is illusion. Illusion is very important; it makes the potential clients aware of who the hell you are.

The big problem with the new agencies is that you need an

accountant and a lawyer – two of the most important people in the world. When people start agencies they forget about that and they think in terms of, Well, I can write and this other guy can draw. Not so. It's a business of an accountant who has some clout at a bank and a lawyer who is willing to go along with you. If you make it with a lawyer and an accountant you're in business.

You can make money right from the word go in advertising. I know of an agency that doesn't have a single account and they're making money. They do special projects. Ten thousand here on a project, twenty thousand a year there. Two guys and a girl – no overhead, no production headaches. They do special projects because nobody will trust them with a full account. When Ron and I were at Bates we made a lot of money for ourselves farming out our talent on special projects. It was written in my contract that I could do freelance work. It was at Bates where I learned that I never wanted to do political advertising.

I had a special project to do a campaign for a Philadelphia politician named Arlen Spector. 'When do I get to see Arlen Spector?' I asked. 'You don't.' Spector was a district attorney in Philadelphia, running for mayor. He wanted New York advertising but he had placed through a Philadelphia agency. I complained about not being able to see Arlen Spector. 'Are you crazy?' his people said. 'Nobody gets to meet Arlen Spector. We can't even see him.' 'All right,' I said, 'what's Arlen Spector for?' 'Arlen Spector is for getting elected.' 'All right,' I said, 'what's Arlen Spector against?' 'Arlen Spector is against losing.' I did the campaign, but Arlen Spector lost.

Everybody is doing freelance. My people are doing it. I walked into an art director's office the other day and saw something for Schaefer Beer. I said to myself, son of a gun,

I didn't realize we got the account. I was all set to have a drink on it until I realized the guy was doing something for Schaefer on a freelance basis.

I've been very lucky in this business. My first job was my best job. Daniel & Charles was great and is great. It was crazy, sheer lunacy but it was fun. Working for Shep at Delehanty was fun, too, although sometimes people thought we were going to kill each other. I really began thinking about having my own place when I was working for Shep.

When I left Shep to go to Bates my mind was made up, and like Bates was the clincher. I knew after a while at Bates that if I wanted to stay in the advertising business and make a living and be able to hold my head up about my work, I knew that I had to have my own place. When Bates hired me they were trying to buy some of that alleged magic, some of that Doyle, Dane touch. What Bates and a lot of other agencies haven't caught on to is that it doesn't hurt to be born Italian or Jewish in the streets of the City of New York. You can't buy the experience. The copywriter is in disgrace today if he was born in a suburb of Boston, of a fairly well-to-do family.

A guy I'll call Churchill convinced me that if I wanted to keep my sanity I had to have my own place. This guy Churchill was famed throughout Bates for having written the headline for some stuff called Certs – 'Two mints in one.' Certs is a minty breath thing and Churchill wrote this famous commercial: There are two girls arguing and one girl says Certs is a breath mint and the other girl says it's a candy mint. The announcer comes on and says, 'Girls, girls, don't argue. It's two mints, two mints, two mints in one.' Oh, it's a fantastic commercial, it is some claim to fame in the history of man. Two mints in one.

Churchill also did the head cutaway and put hammers

inside it for Anacin. Churchill produced the famous nose test where you're told to send your sinuses to Arizona and if you can't get your simuses on a plane try Dristan. Great stuff. I once wrote a memo up at Bates about Certs: 'Listening to the meeting today I've come up with the theme that "Certs Cures Cancer." I'd like to proceed with some storyboards on this theme.' That memo almost caused a fistfight at Bates.

A terrific business, the advertising business. Young kids pounding on doors trying to get in. Agencies starting, folding. The new agencies are getting hot, the older ones are getting hardening of the arteries. I make a good living from advertising. I like to think the work I do is good – I know damn well it sells the product because my clients wouldn't have anything to do with me if I didn't move the product. I don't have to resort to 'two mints in one,' or 'fights headaches three ways,' or 'builds strong bodies twelve ways.' I don't get too much sleep but I don't cry myself to sleep either, the way a lot of guys do. I don't kid anybody, least of all myself. I really love the business. There are some bad scenes you read about in this book. The things that are wrong in advertising would be wrong in any business. But don't get the impression that I don't dig the business. I really do. I could only write about the advertising game this way because I really do love it. Most people say, 'This is a terrible business.' They throw up their hands and go home to Rye at night and forget about it. There are ugly people in advertising, real charlatans, but there are good people, too. And good advertising. And I honestly believe that advertising is the most fun you can have with your clothes on.

About the Author

Jerry Della Femina has worked in advertising for almost fifty years. He started when he was sixteen years old and is currently chairman and CEO of Della Femina Rothschild Jeary and Partners.